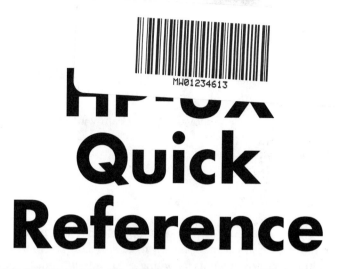

HP-UX
Quick
Reference

OnWord Press Development Team
with Jim Rice

ONWORD®
PRESS

HP-UX Quick Reference

By the OnWord Press Development Team with Jim Rice

Published by:
OnWord Press
2530 Camino Entrada
Santa Fe, NM 87505-4835 USA

Copyright ©1994 OnWord Press
First Edition, 1994
SAN 694-0269

10 9 8 7 6 5 4 3 2 1

Printed in the United States of America

Library of Congress Cataloging-in-Publication Data
    OnWord Press Development Team with Rice, Jim
    HP-UX Quick Reference
    Includes index.
    1. Hewlett-Packard's HP-UX (operating system) I. Title
    92-61887

ISBN 0-934605-23-8

Trademarks

Warning and Disclaimer

About the Author

Jim Rice is a Technical Consultant with Hewlett-Packard's Professional Services Organization. He's been working with UNIX operating systems and windowing environments since 1983. He specializes in helping users understand and work with open systems environments. Jim also serves on the Board of Directors for the InterWorks Workstation User's Group. Over 5000 members strong, InterWorks promotes the understanding and effective use of Hewlett-Packard workstations.

Thanks for the Help

Thanks to the entire OnWord Press team, including Dan Raker, Frank Conforti, Margaret Burns, Carol Leyba, and David Talbott, for their direction and hard work which ensured a quality finished product. Thanks also to John Thompson for his spot reviews and the constructive criticism of my work.

This book is dedicated to my wife Marie and my children Jase, Pat, and Anne.

Jim Rice
November 1993

OnWord Press

OnWord Press is dedicated to the fine art of professional documentation. In addition to the author who developed the material for this book, other members of the OnWord Press team contributed to making this book.

Dan Raker, President
Kate Hayward, Publisher
Gary Lange, Associate Publisher
David Talbott, Acquisitions Director
Frank Conforti, Managing Editor
Carol Leyba, Production Manager
Clint Hicks and Laura Sanchez, Project Editors
Margaret Burns, Production Editor
Lynne Egensteiner, Cover Designer
Catherine Hemenway, Copyeditor
Tierney Tully and Bob Leyba, Production Assistants

Book Production

This book was written on an HP 9000/710 with a 1.03Gb drive and 32Mb of memory, an HP Vectra 486/66DX2, and a Packard Bell 386SX PC-compatible laptop. Text files were converted between DOS and UNIX formats with the HP-UX utilities, ux2dos and dos2ux and imported to Ventura Publisher v4.1.1. Picture files were processed using PaintShop Pro. The cover was designed by Lynne Egensteiner, using QuarkXpress 3.11 and Aldus FreeHand 3.0. Color separations for the cover were prepared by Spectrum Color of Colorado. The book was printed from PostScript files by Edwards Brothers, Inc.

Contents

3 Working with Text Files

4 Using Electronic Mail

5 Customizing the HP VUE Environment

6 101 Commonly Used UNIX Commands

Introduction to Hewlett-Packard's HP-UX and This Book

Welcome to the HP-UX Quick Reference, our guide to the important parts of the HP-UX operating environment. In this introduction to the HP-UX environment, we'll tell you a little bit about your workstation environment, including information about its developer, Hewlett-Packard (HP). We'll also let you know more about our intended audience for the book, and we'll discuss some of the textual and graphical conventions that we use.

About HP-UX: UNIX with Quality and Standards Built In

The Hewlett-Packard HP-UX operating system represents one of the highest quality, standards-based UNIX operating systems in the marketplace. Originally released in 1983, HP-UX represents one of the largest installed base of UNIX-based workstations and servers in the world today.

All computers that run the HP-UX operating system are referred to as the 9000 family of computers. The 9000 family contains four series of computers, the 300, 400, 700, and 800 series systems. The 300 and 400 series systems are workstations based on the Motorola microprocessor and are maintained today to provide investment protection for the owners of this series of workstations. The series 700 is a workstation series based on Hewlett-Packard's PA-RISC architecture. This workstation, introduced in the spring of 1991, has maintained its position as one of fastest UNIX workstations in the marketplace. The final collection of computers, in the 9000 family, is the 800 series. The 800 series is a PA-RISC-based server family that includes features not commonly found in workstations. These include multi-processing, power failure recovery, and extended disk management facilities. Introduced in 1986, the series 800 family represents one of the first RISC/UNIX-based computer products available.

In this book we'll be talking about the latest release of the HP-UX operating system, release 9.0. HP-UX is based on the AT&T System V operating system (SVID2 interface specifications), with many of the most popular extensions from the University of California, Berkeley, version of UNIX (BSD4.3). HP-UX also contains the features required to make it compliant with the IEEE POSIX definitions (1003.1, 1003.2, and 1003.2), the X/Open's™ XPG4, the FIPS 151-1, and the OSF Application Environment Specification (AES). In other words, HP-UX is about as standard as you can get. Hewlett-Packart is committed to keeping HP-UX as compliant with the available standards as possible, without sacrificing the quality that its users have come to expect.

On top of the HP-UX operating system is the HP VUE graphical user interface (GUI). HP VUE is based on the OSF/Motif look and feel definition, which is endorsed by all major workstation vendors today. Currently at release 3.01, it provides a uniform working environment for all applications running on the system. Included in the HP VUE environment are a number of productivity tools that are used to perform routine daily chores for the user, including electronic mail handling, printer control, file management, and more.

About Hewlett-Packard: UNIX with the Power of PA-RISC

The Hewlett-Packard Company traces its roots back to the meeting of its founders during the 1930s. Bill Hewlett and Dave Packard met while both were doing their undergraduate work at Stanford University. Upon graduation, Dave Packard went to work in the Vacuum Tube Research Department of the General Electric Company and Bill went on to do graduate work at Stanford and later at Massachusetts Institute of Technology. But their work brought them back together when Dave returned to Stanford to work on another degree and Bill returned to Stanford on a research fellowship.

As an outgrowth of work from Bill's thesis on resistance-tuned oscillators, Bill and Dave became convinced that they had a product that could be built more reliably and cheaply than other comparable products on the market. Hence, they received their first order from Walt Disney Studios to build eight of these new oscillators for use with a new movie that Disney was working on called Fantasia. The only thing left was the famous toss of a coin. The coin fell to favor the name Hewlett-Packard Company instead of the Packard-Hewlett Company.

Starting as an instrumentation and measurement company, HP introduced its first computer products in 1966 to do sophisticated instrumentation control. By 1972, HP began shipping its first general-purpose computers for business and commercial applications. In 1986, HP began shipping computers based on its reduced instruction set computing (RISC) called the HP-Precision Architecture (HP-PA) and HP's HP-UX operating system. These systems were first used with commercial clients and applications.

After acquiring Apollo Computer in 1989, HP took some of the best aspects of the Apollo PRISM RISC architecture to enhance HP-PA and developed its first HP-PA RISC desktop workstation, the 9000 series 700 computer. Building on nearly 10 years of successfully shipping Motorola-based workstations, HP has become a leader in the shipment of RISC- and UNIX-based systems.

Who Should Read This Book

This book is intended for all those who want quick answers to their questions about Hewlett-Packard workstations running HP-UX. Whether you're a broker working on an HP-UX workstation network, or a manager shepherding a group of engineers who rely on HP workstations, or just a lone user with an HP workstation and a dream, we think you'll find that this book offers you the tools and knowledge you need to get the most productive work out of your software and hardware investment.

This book is for you if

○ You are new to the UNIX environment and know little or nothing about open systems or a GUI working environment.

○ You are experienced in UNIX, but new to a GUI working environment.

○ You are UNIX- and GUI-experienced, but need a fast course in HP-UX.

○ You need to know more about the most common UNIX commands supported by the HP-UX systems.

About This Book

This book is organized into two major sections. The first deals with the HP VUE graphical user interface. This section is made up of five chapters covering accessing your workstation, file operations, electronic mail, text editing, and customization. The second covers 101 of the most commonly used UNIX commands.

What We Mean: Conventions Used in This Book

In order to keep confusion to a minimum, we use the following conventions throughout this book:

```
This font is used for examples of com-
mands, prompts, and user responses. What
you see in this font is what you should
be seeing on the screen.
```

<Keyname> indicates a named key on the keyboard; for instance, <Return>.

Italics in this font are used for mandatory command options and arguments.

[Brackets] are used for optional command options and arguments.

⏎ is the symbol for the <Return> or <Enter> key.

Where command switches may be used together in the command, they will be indicated together in the command usage description. For example, the -a and -l switches for the list directory command can be entered separately or as the single switch -al.

"Quotes" surround new terms and words that have meanings in HP-UX not common to ordinary English.

First Letter Capitalization is used for menu names and selections and button names.

ALL CAPS are used for the names of mouse buttons. Mouse actions may be noted by button name rather than position, to wit: SELECT is the left mouse button, ADJUST is the middle button, and MENU is the right-most. (The order of the mouse buttons can be reversed for the left-handed use. However, this book assumes the default mouse configuration for the sake of simplicity.)

When you are directed to take an action with the mouse, the following syntax is used:

Click SELECT, or simply SELECT, means to press and release the SELECT button. For instance, an instruction to "SELECT Find then Replace" would mean to click SELECT on the Find then Replace button.

Double-click means to quickly press and release the named mouse button two times.

> ✏ *NOTE: If the mouse button name is not specified, SE-LECT is intended.*

Press SELECT means to press and hold the SELECT, or the left mouse, button.

Drag (selection) means to place the pointer on the selection, press a mouse button, move the selection to another position, and release the mouse button.

> ✏ *NOTE: This icon is used for important information that could be missed if included in normal body text.*

> ✔ *TIP: This icon indicates a shortcut or recommended method of operation.*

> ☞ *WARNING: This icon warns of a procedure that can at least cause major inconvenience to the user.*

Some Common Symbolic Notations

The following symbols may be used in command entry and in writing or editing scripts and data files.

> ✏ *NOTE: Some of these symbols have additional meanings when used with certain commands.*

<|> The vertical slash is a pipe symbol used to run the output of a command through another command or filter. For instance, `ls -l | more` would list the current directory in long form. It would be piped through the `more` filter so that the display would stop when the screen is full, rather than letting the top of the list scroll off the screen.

<*> An asterisk may be used as a wildcard to manipulate files. For instance, `mv *.letters /pcstuff` would move all files beginning with anything and ending with `.letters` to `/pcstuff`.

<?> A question mark may be used to manipulate files to wildcard specific positions in a filename. For instance, find reports. qtr?9? would find all such files as reports.qtr391, reports.qtr492, etc.

<#> The pound sign is most often used to turn a line in a script or data file into a comment, as for example, #this is the external drive.

<-> The hyphen is commonly used as a switch in UNIX command notation. For instance, ls would merely list the files in the current working directory. However, ls -l would list the files in long form, showing such characteristics as size, last modification, and type.

<&> An ampersand at the end of a command (separated with a space) causes the command to run in background, thus allowing you to use your shell window for other things while that command is running.

<~> A tilde may be used in the beginning of a pathname to signify your home directory. For instance, if your home directory is /users/jim, and you wish to run a script in /users/jim/bin, you could key the command as:

$ ~/bin/script_name <Enter>

You can also switch to another user's home directory by using the tilde with the cd command. For instance, to switch to bills' home directory, key in:

$ cd ~bill <Enter>

<Esc> This key prefaces certain command options in tools such as the vi editor.

<Control>+<C> This terminates an active process.

<Control>+<U> This erases an entire command line (providing that <Enter> has not been pressed).

Fundamental Operations

Fundamentals

The following operations are fundamental to accessing and using the HP Workstation capabilities.

Logging In

"Logging in" is the process of gaining access to your HP workstation system. Soon after you turn the machine on, you must supply it with your username, which lets the machine know who you are, and your password, which serves to prove that you're really who you claim to be.

When you are added to the system as an authorized user, an account is created for you. This account identifies who you are (your username and what groups you belong to), what the initial password for your account is, and where your personal data storage is located. Your account information is important because it is used to determine what parts of the computer's filesystem you are allowed to have access to and what type of services (such as electronic mail and printing) you will have at your disposal once you are logged in to your system.

The HP VUE Login Window.

Once you have an account on your system, you are ready to log in. When you sit down at your workstation, you'll encounter a login display. The login welcomes you to your workstation and asks you to enter your username and password. You can log in to your computer by using the mouse to point at the Login field and then press the left mouse button. This highlights the field and you can start typing your username. Once you've typed your username, you can either press the <Enter> key on your keyboard to advance to the Password field, or you can use the mouse to highlight the field and then type your password.

> *NOTE:* *While typing in your password, you won't see the letters or numbers in the display. This is to ensure that nobody looking over your shoulder will be able to see your password. It's OK, the computer knows what you're typing.*

At the bottom of this screen you'll notice four buttons. They're labeled "OK," "Clear," "Options," and "Help." The OK button is pressed once you've finished typing in your username and password to tell the computer you're done typing. (You can accomplish the same thing by pressing < Enter > after you've typed in your password). The Clear button is used to erase anything in the Login or Password fields on the display so you can enter your personal information on a clean slate. The Options button is used for selecting different login options such as telling your computer to use a different language (e.g., German or French), to turn the graphical user interface off, etc. The final button is the Help button. If you find you're having trouble getting logged into your workstation, try pressing this button and then read the help window before you look for a more experienced person to beg help from.

The HP VUE Workspace Manager

Almost all of the different parts of HP VUE can be accessed from the HP VUE Workspace Manager's Front Panel. The Front Panel is the bar that you see located along the bottom of the window as soon as you log into your workstation. It can be thought of as the dashboard to your car. It provides you with some useful information and allows you to push buttons to make things happen. In the case of HP VUE, you are presented with information like the time of day, date, and an e-mail indicator. The Front Panel also gives you buttons and menus to access a number of different applications provided with your workstation. These applications include a help system, tools to customize your Workspace, terminal emulators, and a File Manager.

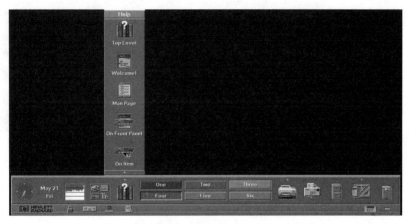

The HP VUE Workspace Manager.

Logging Out

To log out at the end of your work session, use the mouse
to point at and select the Exit button found on the bottom
right corner of your Workspace Manager.

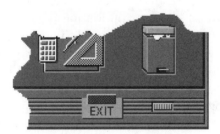

The HP VUE Logout button.

The system may ask you to confirm your logout; press the
OK button if it does.

If you need to take any further action before you log out of
your workstation, you'll see a dialog box on your display.

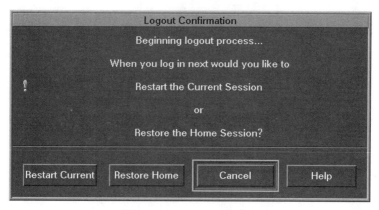

The HP VUE Logout dialog.

The dialog box gives you two options. You can choose to have the HP VUE Window Manager restart all the applications that you are running currently the next time you log in. Alternately, you can have HP VUE just start up the applications you've defined as your Home Session the next time you log in. You can read more about defining your Home Session in chapter 5, "Customizing Your Environment." The logout process continues after you have chosen one of these options. You will know you've logged out when you see the HP VUE login window appear.

Working with Pop-up Menus

An alternative way to invoke some of HP VUE's functions is through the pop-up menu on the desktop. To access this pop-up menu, move the mouse pointer to an open space on the background of the desktop and press the right mouse button. A menu will be displayed that gives you access to some of the basic Window Manager functions.

The HP VUE Desktop pop-up menu.

Working with Windows

A window is a special area on the Workspace, belonging to a program or application. All of your text entry and editing tasks take place within a program's window. With few exceptions, a window will have a number of attributes that are common regardless of the program or application that's running in it. These common attributes are what allow you to control where the window is placed on the desktop, how big the window is, and whether it's fully visible or in an icon.

A window is made up of a number of different areas. These are the input area, title bar, resize handles, window menu button, window menu, minimize button, and maximize button.

The largest part of a window is the input area. This is where you see text areas, buttons, scroll bars, etc. This is the area of your window that represents the user interface for the application that's running. It is the part of your window in which you're likely to spend most of your time.

At the top of a window is its title bar. The title bar identifies the application—and possibly the document—to which the

Fundamentals

window belongs. The title bar can be used to position the window on the desktop. This is done by moving the mouse pointer to the title bar, pressing the left mouse button, and dragging the window to where you want it on the desktop before you release the mouse button.

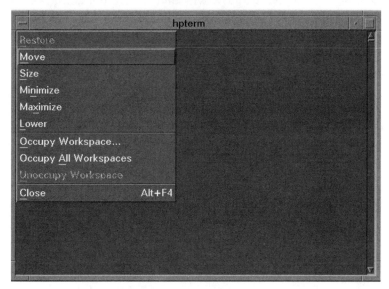

hpterm

Restore
Move
Size
Minimize
Maximize
Lower
Occupy Workspace...
Occupy All Workspaces
Unoccupy Workspace
Close   Alt+F4

A basic HP VUE window.

You can change a window's size by dragging in its resize handles; these handles appear at each corner and each edge of a window. They look like a picture frame around the window. You can change the visible size of your application window with the mouse by clicking and dragging the edge or corner of your window to where you want it.

The window menu can be viewed by clicking the left mouse button on the window menu button—the button to the left of the title bar with the small horizontal line in it. By bringing up this menu, you'll be able to select one of a number of functions that you can perform on your window, such as Close, Minimize, Move, or Lower.

You can have several windows open on the screen at once. These windows can belong to one or several applications. However, even though all windows contain actively running programs, only one window can be active at a time. An active window is the one that will receive all keyboard and mouse inputs. The active window will have a different color border than the rest of the windows on the desktop. You can make any window active by moving the mouse pointer into it and pressing the left mouse button.

Working with Icons

Since you may be running a number of applications on your desktop at any given time, you'll want to minimize the amount of clutter on your desktop by placing some of your windows into icons. An icon is a small graphic that represents a window, or collection of windows, that belongs to an application. You can place a window into an icon by using the left mouse button to click on the Minimize button on the window border. This button is located immediately to the right of the title bar and contains a small raised dot. Another way you could place a window into an icon is by selecting the Minimize item from the window's pull-down menu.

HP VUE icons.

Once you've minimized a window to an icon, you might decide that you want to get the window back. This is accomplished by using the mouse to point at the icon and pressing the left mouse button to view the icon's menu. One of the items in the icon menu is Restore. By selecting this menu item, you'll restore the windows from the icon to their original form. A quicker way to restore a window is to quickly double-click the left mouse button on the icon.

2

File and Folder Operations

This chapter deals with commands that you can perform using the HP VUE File Manager. The File Manager is a tool that you can use to navigate around your workstation's filesystem. Using the File Manager, you can create, copy, move, open, and delete files and folders. This chapter includes the basics of how to use the File Manager to perform these and other HP VUE actions.

Viewing a Directory with the HP VUE File Manager

File Manager

You can begin using the HP VUE File Manager by selecting the graphic that looks like a file cabinet on the HP VUE Front Panel. Select the icon by moving the mouse pointer over the graphic and pressing the left mouse button once.

The icon used to open the HP VUE File Manager.

Once you've selected the HP VUE File Manager icon, the HP VUE File Manager window opens to display a graphical view of the files and subdirectories in your home directory.

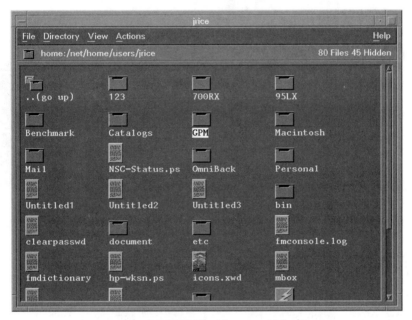

The HP VUE File Manager Window.

Inside the window borders (that we learned about in the last chapter) the HP VUE File Manager has three basic work areas: the Menu bar, the Status Line, and the Directory Viewing area. You can see an example of these areas in the preceding illustration.

Starting from the bottom of the window you can see icons representing files and directories. Directories are represented by folder icons, and simple data files have icons that look like pieces of paper. The name of a file or folder is shown below its icon. You may see other icons that look like sunsets, firecrackers, crumpled pages, and other items. These are data files that the HP VUE File Manager recognizes and associates with actions that you might want to take. We'll discuss actions in more detail later.

As with many other HP VUE windows, a scroll bar is provided because the contents of the display area may not all be visible at once. Use the scroll bar to see more files in this directory.

Above the Display Area is a Status Line. The Status Line shows you the name of the computer and the pathname to the directory you're viewing.

Above the Status Line are the HP VUE File Manager menus. These menus are used to perform operations on files or directories. They can also be used to configure the look and feel of the HP VUE File Manager windows. These menus are covered in more detail later in this chapter.

Files and Folders

Changing the Directory Display

File Manager ➠ *Change Directory View* ➠

When using the HP VUE File Manager, you may want to change the directory that you're viewing or working in. This is done in one of three ways, by:

O Using the Directory menu

O Changing the Status Line

O Selecting a directory icon

You can change the current working directory by using the pull-down menu titled "Directory." By selecting this menu, you are presented with options to move "Up" one directory level, move to your "Home" directory, "Change To" a direc-

tory you have been in recently, or "Fast Change To" a
directory pathname that you type in.

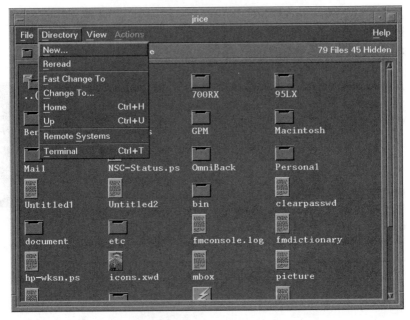

The HP VUE File Manager Directory menu.

Another way you can change the current directory is by
pointing the mouse at the Status Line of the HP VUE File
Manager. While pointing at the Status line, simply click the
left mouse button once. This changes the status line into a
text edit line into which you type the pathname of the
directory that you'd like to view. The directory view will
change as soon as you press the <Enter> key. If you haven't
tried it yet, this is exactly what the Fast Change To menu item
in the Directory menu does for you.

The last way to change the directory view is probably the simplest, though not the fastest. Use the mouse pointer to point at and select one of the directories in the directory view area. By double-clicking on a directory, you will change the directory that you're currently viewing to the one that you've just selected. This allows you to traverse down into subdirectories. By selecting the directory labeled ".." (go up) you can return to the parent of your current directory.

If you want to open a new, additional window with a view of one of the other directories in your current view area, highlight the directory with a single click and then select the item from the Action menu titled "OpenNewView." This opens a second HP VUE File Manager window and leaves your original view unchanged.

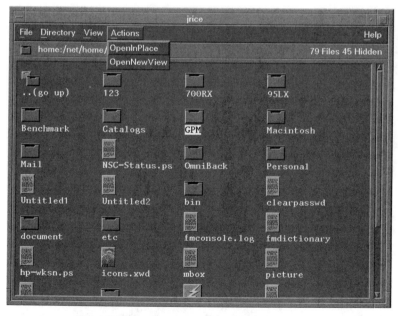

The HP VUE File Manager Actions menu.

Copying Files

File Manager ➡ *File menu* ➡ *Copy*

The HP VUE File Manager provides a couple of ways to copy highlighted files to another filename or directory in your system.

You can copy a file by first highlighting it in the file viewing area, then selecting Copy... from the File menu. A dialog box appears asking for the filename to be used for the copy. This new name can be a unique filename in the current directory view or a complete pathname to the new file's location.

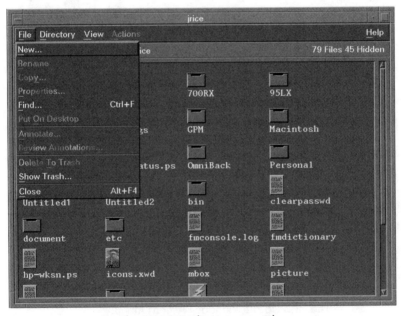

The HP VUE File Manager File menu.

Another way to make a copy of a file is by dragging the file from one File Manager view to another. Once you have two File Manager windows open, displaying the source and destination directories, use the mouse pointer to highlight the source file that you wish to copy. Once you've highlighted this file in the source directory view, drag it to the other File Manager view while holding down the <Control> key on your keyboard. This will make a copy of the selected file in the new directory, using the same filename.

You can highlight and copy multiple files from one directory to another by holding the <Control> key down while you select the files in the source directory.

> ☞ *WARNING: If you don't hold the <Control> key down while you drag the files from one File Manager view to another, the files will be MOVED. The file will no longer exist in the original file view, only in the destination.*

In addition to moving files around on your local computer, the HP VUE File Manager has the ability to copy files to another computer's filesystem. This is done in exactly the same way you copy files to another directory. Only in this instance, the File Manager view—or the destination file-name—is prefaced with "hostname:" before the destination pathname.

Creating a Folder

File Manager ➡ *File menu* ➡ *New...*

This command allows you to create subdirectories to suit your needs. The new subdirectory is placed within the current directory, that is, the one whose contents are shown in the file view.

Customizing the File Display

File Manager ➡ View menu ➡ Set Preferences...

This command brings up a pop-up window. Here you can specify exactly how you want files to appear in the file view.

Customizing the HP VUE File Manager display.

Once you change the File Manager preferences for the current file view, you may want to change the preferences for all future HP VUE File Managers that you invoke. To do this, select the Save Settings... item from the View menu.

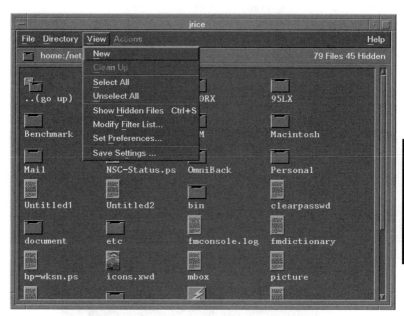

Saving the current HP VUE File Manager preferences.

Deleting Files and Directories

File Manager ➡ *File menu* ➡ *Delete to Trash*

The Delete to Trash command removes selected files or directories and puts them into the Trash Can. You can also place items in the Trash Can by dragging them to the Trash Can icon on the HP VUE Front Panel.

Using the Delete to Trash feature of the HP VUE environment doesn't actually remove the files from your computer's system until you empty the Trash Can. The files or directories are simply renamed until you select the Trash Can icon on the HP VUE Workspace Manager and use its File menu to select the files again and request that they be removed.

Until you empty the Trash Can, you can retrieve files from it. Select the Trash Can icon on the Front Panel, select the file(s) you'd like to retrieve, and then, from the Trash Can's File menu, select Restore. This will move the file you've selected back to the directory it was deleted from.

The HP VUE Trash Can dialog box.

Finding Files and Folders

File Manager ➡ *File menu* ➡ *Find...*

The HP VUE File Manager offers a File menu item that you can use to locate a file or folder in the filesystem. Choosing Find... displays a pop-up window in which you will enter your search criterion for the items you want the File Manager to find.

Enter the file or directory name into the File or Directory Name edit field to tell the File Manager what you would like to find.

You can specify where to begin looking for the file or directory by entering the appropriate directory pathname in the Search Directory edit field. (The default is from the current directory shown in the File Manager view.)

Files and Folders

The Find dialog window. You can search for files by name or contents.

If you are interested in files that contain some tidbit of information, you can search within files to locate the ones that contain a certain piece of data. This is done by typing the data on the File Contents edit field.

When you're happy with the search criterion you've entered, click the Start button to begin searching. The files that match your criterion will be shown in the Found files list seen near the bottom of the dialog box.

Double-clicking on a file or directory displayed in the Files Found panel will bring up a new HP VUE File Manager view displaying that file or directory.

Invoking an Action from the File Manager

File Manager ➡Action menu

A file or directory that has File Manager "actions" has some operations or an application associated with it. When the file or directory is highlighted, the Action menu will contain a list of the actions that can be performed on it. The list will change, depending on the actions that have been defined for the particular file or directory that you're working on. For example, a text file will have actions defined to Open or Print. A directory will have actions defined to OpenInPlace or OpenNewView.

You may invoke a File Manager action by selecting the file or directory that you'd like to work on. Then, pull down the Action menu and select the action that you'd like to perform.

 TIP: The first item in the Action menu may be invoked by simply double-clicking on the file or directory in question.

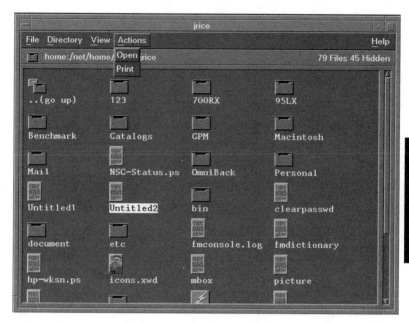

An HP VUE File Manager Action menu.

Renaming Files

File Manager ➥ File menu ➥ Rename

You can change the name of a file by highlighting it in the File Manager view window and then choosing the Rename item from the File menu. Choosing Rename will change the highlighted item name in the File Manager view to an edit field. In this field you can enter the new name of the file or directory.

TIP: *A shortcut to changing the name of the file or directory is to highlight its icon in the File Manager view. Then, using the mouse, point at the name of the icon for the item and press the left mouse button again. This will also cause the icon name to change to an edit field, without having to pull down the file menu.*

Selecting a Printer

HP VUE Workspace Manager ➠*Printer button*

While at your workstation, you often have to print something out. When you do, you may have several printers available. These printers may be connected to your local computer, to other computers on the network, or directly connected to the network itself. No matter how they are connected, the question is, how do you find out what printers are available, and how can you use them once you know?

On the HP VUE Front Panel, you will see a small icon that looks like a printer; above this icon is a small triangular arrow. Pressing on this arrow displays a pull-up menu with icons for all of the printers available to your system.

 TIP: *If you'd like to have this list of printers displayed all the time, you can move this menu to any place on the display by moving the mouse pointer to the menu's title bar and dragging it to a convenient place on your desktop for later use.*

Once you know what printers are available, you can print a file to a specific printer by dragging the file's icon from the File Manager view to the printer's icon. If you don't use the pull-up menu and drag your file's icon to the printer icon located on the front panel, the file will be printed on your workstation's default printer. See your system administrator to find out which printer this is.

> ☞ *NOTE: You may have seen a Print item in the Action menu for some of the files in the File Manager. If you choose this item to print your highlighted file, rather than dragging it to a printer icon, you will print your file on your workstation's default printer.*

Once you are done printing, you may not want to clutter your desktop with the printer menu anymore. You can close the pull-up menu by pressing on the small triangular arrow located below the last printer on the menu.

Files and Folders

Changing the Properties of a File

File Manager ➡ File menu ➡ Properties

HP-UX filesystem objects, such as files and directories, have properties associated with them. These properties include:

○ The username of the person who owns the file

○ The name of the group of users that the object belongs to

○ The type of object

○ The permissions that users have with regard to the object

○ Other information such as modification dates and the object's size

Selecting the Properties item from the File menu opens a dialog box that lets you view and change some of the properties for the object you have selected. If you are the owner of the file, you will be able to change the object's owner, its group, and the permissions. The permissions for an object describe who may read, write over, and execute the object. If you do not own the object, you will only be allowed to view its current properties.

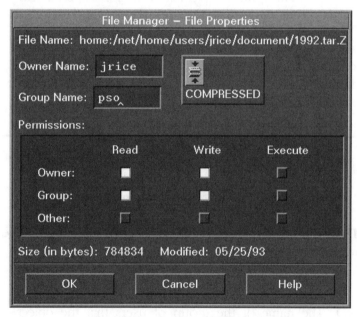

The File Properties... dialog box.

In the preceding illustration, the File Properties dialog box displays information specific to the marked file, such as its size, owner, and when it was last modified. Note that the information in the dialog box applies to the file marked in the File Manager view when you selected the File Properties menu item.

3

Working with Text Files

Working with text is one of the most common activities that any of us do on a computer. We may be running sophisticated page layout programs, complex engineering simulations, writing programs to run on the system, or preparing a letter to send to Mom. Regardless of the activity we're involved in, we are going to be working, in some way, with text.

In this chapter, we'll be dealing with the graphical text editor that's included in the HP VUE desktop environment, the HP Vuepad. While there are literally hundreds of possible editors that you might consider using, few are as simple to use as the HP Vuepad.

Starting the HP Vuepad Text Editor

HP VUE Front Panel ➡ *Select icon or Action*

The HP VUE environment includes a graphical text editor called the HP Vuepad. The editor can be invoked from any number of places in your desktop environment. These include the HP VUE Front Panel icon, the HP VUE File Manager, the electronic mail interface, or almost any shell prompt.

From the HP VUE desktop, you can start the HP Vuepad editor by pressing its icon, located in the small gray bar at the bottom of the Front Panel. This icon looks like a pencil writing on a piece of paper.

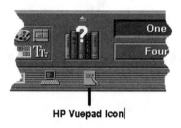

HP Vuepad Icon|

The HP Vuepad icon.

To edit a particular document, start the HP Vuepad through the HP VUE File Manager. Select the file you want to edit in the File Manager window and choose the Open item in the Action pull-down menu. This will launch the HP Vuepad editor, with the selected file already open.

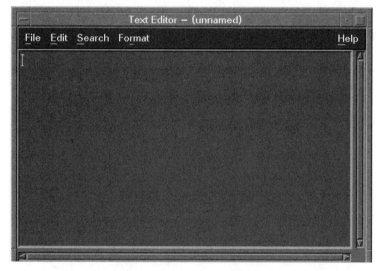

The HP Vuepad text editor.

The HP Vuepad editor is made up of two basic areas, the menus and the text edit area. The menus are found along the top of the edit window and are titled "File," "Edit," "Search," "Format," and "Help." You can pull down any one of these menus by pointing your mouse at the name of the menu and pressing the left mouse button to select it. The text edit area is found immediately below the menu bar and is where all text editing on your file will take place.

Once you have the HP Vuepad editor open, you can place your text entry cursor (the cursor that looks like a tall, skinny capital "I") anyplace in the file shown in your text edit area. Simply place the mouse pointer anywhere in the text and press the left mouse button. Once you've placed your text edit cursor in the file, you can start typing away.

HP Vuepad: Opening a Text File

HP Vuepad Text Editor ➡ *File* ➡ *Open*

Once you have the HP Vuepad editor running, you may want to open a new file for editing. You can do this by choosing the Open item from the File pull-down menu. Choosing this item will bring up a dialog box that allows you to browse through your directories and select the file that you want to edit.

Text Files

A sample Open File dialog from the HP Vuepad Editor.

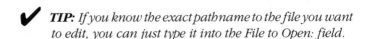 **TIP:** *If you know the exact pathname to the file you want to edit, you can just type it into the File to Open: field.*

Once the name of the file is displayed in the File to Open: field, press the OK button on the bottom of the dialog box to open the file in the editor window.

HP Vuepad: Including Text from Other Files

HP Vuepad Text Editor ➡ *File* ➡ *Include*

The HP Vuepad offers two methods of including an existing text file into the document you are currently working on. To include a file use the Include... item in the File menu, or drag the file's icon from an HP VUE File Manager window into the HP Vuepad editor window. In either case, the file will be inserted at the current insertion cursor's position.

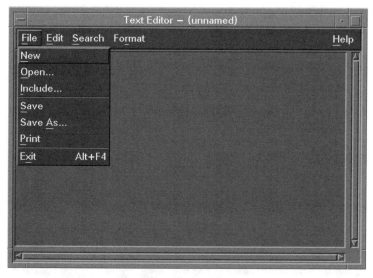

The File pull-down menu.

HP Vuepad: Editing Text

HP Vuepad Text Editor ➡ *Edit*

Of course, we started the HP Vuepad so that we could edit some files. By the time you've gotten around to reading this, you probably have already figured out that you can place the edit cursor anyplace in your text. You do that by using the mouse pointer to select the place to put the insert cursor. After you've placed the insert cursor, you can insert text by typing it in. Alternately, you can delete text by pressing the < Backspace > key to remove anything before the insert cursor. Now, it's time to move on to some trickier editing techniques using the Edit pull-down menu.

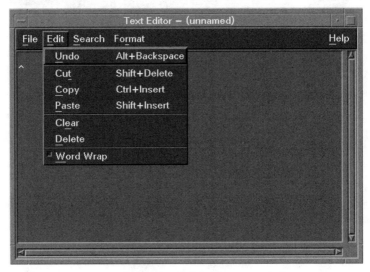

The Edit pull-down menu.

The Edit pull-down menu can be found along the top of the HP Vuepad window. Open this menu by using the mouse pointer to select the menu. The Edit menu includes a number of items: Undo, Cut, Copy, Paste, Clear, Delete, and Word

Wrap. In general, anything you might ever want to do to mangle—uhh... I mean edit—your text.

The Undo option should be pretty obvious. If you've been typing away, deleting text, or trying to insert a file into the document in your editor, you will make a mistake. It happens and it's nothing to get alarmed about. Just use the Undo menu item. The Undo menu item will erase your last action and put things back the way they were.

If you want to move a paragraph from one place in a document to another, you could just backspace over the old one and retype it into the new location. While this may be better than retyping the whole document, there is an easier way.

The next three items in the Edit menu—the Cut, Copy, and Paste commands—are just what we need to make our editing job a little easier. We'll describe how to use these commands in a minute but, before we do, we'll need to talk a little bit about "highlighting" the text that you want to work on.

Highlighting text is how you tell the HP Vuepad editor what part of your document you want to use a command on. For example, if you want to move a sentence from the beginning of a paragraph to the end, you have to indicate what that sentence is. You will do this by highlighting it.

You can highlight any region of your text by using the mouse pointer. By placing your mouse pointer at one end of the area that you'd like to work on, you can press and hold the left mouse button down while you move your mouse pointer to the other end of the area that you'd like to work on. As you move the pointer, you will see the text turn to reverse video. This is called highlighting the text. When you get to the other end of the text region you want to work on, you can release the mouse button.

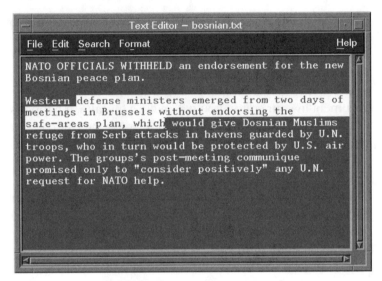

Highlighted text in the HP Vuepad.

Now that you have a region of text highlighted, you can Copy or Cut the text onto the HP Vuepad's paste buffer. The paste buffer is an area in the HP Vuepad's memory that stores the last item that you cut or copied from the text area. Once you have the text you want on the paste buffer, move the text insertion cursor to anyplace in the document (you do remember how to do that, right?) and select the Paste menu item to copy the contents of the paste buffer into the text file at that point.

The last thing on the bottom of the Edit menu is the Word Wrap toggle. By selecting this menu item, you can switch between two different display modes in the text edit area. These two modes determine if the lines that you type in will automatically wrap around to the beginning of the next line as you type beyond the end of the current line. The alternative is to have the view on your file scroll to the right as you continue to type. You can turn Word Wrap off again by choosing the Word Wrap menu item again.

> ✏️ *NOTE:* *When Word Wrap is enabled, the editor doesn't automatically insert a carriage return at the end of the line as you type. It simply displays the single line across two lines in the text edit area. When you save the file, you will be given the option to insert the carriage returns between the lines at that time.*

HP Vuepad: Printing Text

HP Vuepad Text Editor ➡ File ➡ Print

If you are working on a file in the HP Vuepad editor and decide you want to print a copy of your current document, choose the Print item in the File pull-down menu. Choosing this item sends the current document to your default system printer.

HP Vuepad: Spell Checking a Text File

HP Vuepad Text Editor ➡ Search ➡ Spell...

The HP Vuepad editor has a built-in spelling checker that helps to identify words in your text file that have been misspelled. The spelling checker can be invoked by selecting the Spell... item in the Search pull-down menu.

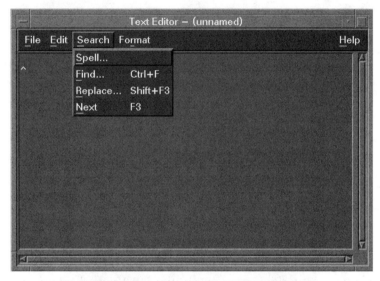

The Search menu showing the Spell... menu item.

The spell checking dialog box in the HP Vuepad.

Once you've selected the spelling checker from the pull-down menu, it scans your document and displays any misspelled words in a dialog box. Enter spelling corrections into this dialog box.

The HP Vuepad doesn't have the world's most sophisticated spelling checker. However, it does a better job of finding the misspelled words than I normally do.

HP Vuepad: Saving a Text File

HP Vuepad Text Editor ➡ *File* ➡ *Save*

If you decide that you'd like to save the file you've been working on in the HP Vuepad editor, you can use the Save or Save As items from the File pull-down menu.

If you choose the Save menu item for a file that already has a disk file associated with it—because you opened it from one, or because you've already saved it to disk once—the disk file is updated with the changes you've made.

If, however, you want to save your file to disk with a new name and choose the Save As... menu button, or if you have never saved this file before, you will be presented with a dialog box asking for the filename you want to use.

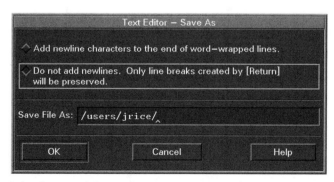

A dialog box used during the Save As process from the HP Vuepad.

HP Vuepad: Exiting

HP Vuepad Text Editor ➡ *File* ➡ *Exit*

Once you've finished working in the HP Vuepad editor and
decide you want to exit, leave the editor by choosing the Exit
menu item from the File pull-down menu.

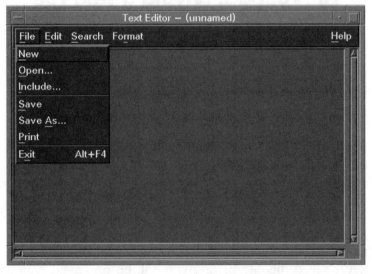

The File pull-down menu showing the Exit menu item.

If you choose to Exit the editor and you've made changes to
your document but haven't saved them, you'll be given a
chance to save your changes before you leave the editor.

4

Using Electronic Mail

Electronic mail is an important element in any UNIX environment. It provides a mechanism for users to communicate with each other and for some applications to communicate with the users. This chapter covers commands to access and control electronic mail (e-mail). All of these commands are found within the basic HP VUE desktop environment.

 NOTE: There is a wide variety of electronic mail interfaces available in the public domain and as commercial products. We'll be discussing the Electronic Mail interface (ELM) included with the HP VUE environment.

Accessing the Electronic Mail Interface

HP VUE Front Panel ➡ *Select the ELM Icon*

To start the electronic mail interface (ELM), select the mail icon from the HP VUE Front Panel.

Mail Icon

The electronic mail icon in the HP VUE Front Panel.

The icon displayed in the Workspace Manager will change to let you know when new e-mail has arrived in your mailbox. You'll see a few new envelopes displayed behind the front envelope graphic. You can invoke the ELM interface by using the mouse pointer to select the mail icon graphic on the HP VUE Workspace Manager.

Mail Icon

The electronic mail interface icon, indicating that new mail has arrived.

An alternate way to start the ELM interface is through the ToolBox menus on the HP VUE Front Panel. Located in the ToolBox pop-up menu is the General Toolbox. This toolbox contains a Communications Toolbox, which offers an action definition for the ELM interface. Selecting this action with the mouse pointer will start the ELM interface.

The ELM interface icon located in the Communications toolbox.

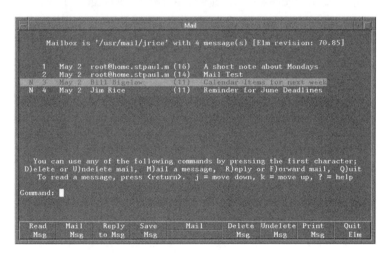

The ELM interface window.

The ELM interface appears when you select the ELM icon from the Front Panel or the ELM action from the Toolbox.

Composing an E-Mail Message

ELM Interface ➡ *Mail Message*

Sending mail to someone is a central function of any electronic mail interface; ELM is no exception. You can begin composing a message to someone by choosing the Mail Message command from the ELM interface menu.

There are three ways to select the Mail Message command in ELM. It can be selected by pressing the special function key <F2>, using the keyboard shortcut for the menu choice <m>, or by using the mouse pointer to select the button on the bottom of the ELM interface window.

Regardless of how you select the Mail Message command, you will be asked who you wish to send the e-mail to, what the subject of the mail is, and if you'd like to send copies to anyone. For example:

```
To: john@myshop.department.com
Subject: A Note about Mondays
Copies To: perry
```

The basic form of an e-mail message is *userid@machine_name*. (See your system administrator for help in addressing e-mail to the outside world via external mail systems such as Internet, UUCPMail, or MCIMail.) Once you have the username/address, you can type it in when ELM asks you for it.

 TIP: *The address lines will accept multiple addressees. For instance, if you want to include two addressees in the To: line, enter each e-mail address, separated by a space.*

Once you've entered the basic information about the message and who it's for, the HP Vuepad text editor appears.

You compose your message using the Vuepad, which we discussed in the last chapter. When you exit the editor, you'll have one last chance to think about what you're sending and who you're sending it to. When you're ready to send your message and you've exited the editor, select the Send Message option and the e-mail will be delivered to its destination.

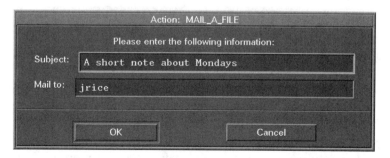

The HP Vuepad text editor.

An alternate way to send someone a message is to first compose the message in a file. Then, from the HP VUE File Manager, highlight the file and drag it to the ELM icon on the Front Panel. When you drop the file on the ELM icon, you'll be given a dialog asking for the Subject of the message you're sending and the person or persons to whom you are sending the file.

The Dialog presented after dropping a file from File Manager onto the ELM icon.

After you enter the subject of the message into the Subject: field and e-mail address of the person or persons into the Mail to: field, you can press OK to send your file on its way. If, before you've pressed the OK, you decide that you really don't want to send the file, you can press the Cancel button on the dialog box.

Deleting a Mail Message

ELM Interface ➡ *Delete Message*

To delete a message, simply highlight the mail in the message summary window of the ELM interface, and then either choose the Delete Message special function key <F5>, press the keyboard shortcut for the function < d >, or use the mouse pointer to select the Delete Message button from the bottom of the window.

> **NOTE:** *Since ELM is a terminal-based mail interface, you can't use the mouse pointer to select the mail message to highlight for deletion. You have to use the arrow keys located in the center keypad to move up and down the mail list to select the message.*

Filing Mail Messages

ELM Interface ➡ *Save Message*

If you prefer to retain electronic, rather than paper, copies of certain mail messages, you can file them within special areas called "mail folders." Folders help you organize your correspondence into collections of messages that are some-how related. You could have a mail folder for memos from your boss, another for meeting minutes, possibly a folder for messages from rabid squirrels, and so on.

If you decide you'd like to save a message, use the arrow keys on the keyboard to highlight it in the mail summary portion of the ELM interface. You can then save the message by using the Save Message command. This command can be selected in one of three ways. You can select the Save Message special function key <F4>, press the keyboard shortcut for this function <s>, or use the mouse pointer to select the button at the bottom of the ELM interface window. You'll be asked to type in the name of the folder that you want to save the mail in.

> 🖎 *NOTE: The default folder name presented is* =/sender. *The* =/ *represents a shorthand version of the folder directory. See Elm Interface—Options for more information about setting the folder directory.*

Printing a Mail Message

ELM Interface ➡ *Print Message*

If you want to print a mail message so that you have a paper copy, choose the Print Message command from the ELM interface. Choosing the Print Message command prints the mail using the print command defined in your ELM interface, Options menu.

To evoke the Print Message command and print a message from your inbox or from one of your mail folders, first highlight the message. You can highlight the message by using the arrow keys on your keyboard to select a mail message from the mail summary window. Once you have highlighted the mail, you can use the Print Message command on it.

E-Mail

Evoke the Print Message command on the highlighted message by either pressing the function key <F7> corresponding to the Print Message button, pressing the keyboard shortcut for the command, <p>, or using the mouse pointer to select the button at the bottom of the ELM interface window. The e-mail message will then be sent to your printer.

Recovering a Message Marked for Deletion

ELM Interface ➡ *Undelete Message*

Sometimes you ask to have a message deleted by mistake. You'll notice that all messages marked for deletion have a "D" to the left of the mail number in the message summary display. If you are currently viewing a message that has been marked for deletion, you will see the notation "[Deleted]" in the upper left corner of the message display.

If you have marked a message for deletion and decide that you'd like to hang on to it for a little longer, you must remove the deletion mark. A deletion mark doesn't affect the mail as long as you are still in the ELM interface. You can remove the mark from the mail by highlighting the message and using the Undelete Message command.

> ☞ *WARNING: Once you leave the ELM interface, all mail marked for deletion is gone forever.*

To remove a deletion mark from a highlighted mail message, use the Undelete Message command. You can evoke the Undelete Message command by choosing the special function key <F6>, pressing the keyboard shortcut <u>, or by using the mouse pointer to select the Undelete Message button at the bottom of the ELM interface window.

Replying to a Mail Message

ELM Interface ➥ *Reply Message*

Sometimes you want to reply to an e-mail message you've received. Maybe you want to RSVP to an invitation for a meeting. Or maybe you want to acknowledge that you received the e-mail you just finished reading. In any event, ELM provides a simple facility for replying to any e-mail message.

To reply to a message you've received, highlight the message in the summary window by scrolling up or down the list using the arrow keys on your keyboard. Once you've highlighted the message you want to reply to, select the Reply Message command.

Select the Reply Message command by pressing the <F3> special function key, pressing the keyboard shortcut key <r>, or by using the mouse to select the Reply To Message button on the bottom of the message summary window. This command is almost identical to the Mail Message command except for the following differences:

○ The To: field will be filled in for you with the return address of the sender of the mail message.

○ You will be given the opportunity to include the original message in the text of the mail that you are sending.

○ The Subject: field will be the same as the original message's subject line, except that it will have the word "Re:" attached to the front of it.

E-Mail

From this point on, follow exactly the same steps that you did when you sent a new message. See ELM Interface ➥ Mail Message.

> 📨 **NOTE:** *If you'd like to include all of the people listed as recipients in the original mail message, as well as the sender, use the keyboard short cut <g> for a Group Reply. There is no ELM interface button for this option.*

Viewing Mail Messages

ELM Interface ➥ Read Message

Once you've received a mail message, you will probably want to read it. Viewing a particular message is easy.

To read any message shown in the mail summary display, highlight the message using the arrow keys on your keyboard. Once you've highlighted the message, you can bring up a view of that message by using the Read Message command.

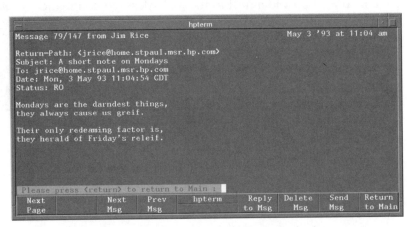

The ELM Interface reading mail using the built-in pager.

The Read Message command can be evoked on any high-lighted mail message by using either the Read Message special function key <F1>, the keyboard shortcut <Enter>, or the mouse pointer to select the Read Message button at the bottom on the ELM interface. The message will be displayed using ELM's built-in pager. Press the space bar on the keyboard to page down through your mail message.

Configuring the ELM Interface

ELM Interface ➡ *Configurations Options*

If you decide that you'd like to change the behavior of the ELM interface, you can do so using the ELM Options menu. Access this menu by using the keyboard shortcut key <o> to change to the ELM Options menu.

```
                              hpterm
                       — Elm Options Editor —

C)alendar file        : /net/home/users/jrice/calendar
D)isplay mail using   : builtin
E)ditor               : /usr/vue/bin/vuepad█
F)older directory     : /net/home/users/jrice/Mail
S)orting criteria     : received
O)utbound mail saved  : /net/home/users/jrice/mbox
P)rint mail using     : pr %s | lp
Y)our full name       : Jim Rice


A)rrow cursor         : OFF
M)enu display         : ON

U)ser level           : 0 (for Beginning User)
N)ames only           : OFF
T)abs to spaces       : OFF

       This is the editor that will be used for sending messages, etc.

Command:
```

The ELM Options menu.

You can change some of the basic configuration options of the ELM interface using the ELM Options menu. Options such as the Folder Directory, the Sorting Criteria, and the printer command are some of the most commonly changed configuration options in ELM.

Adding Username Aliases to ELM

ELM Interface ➥ *Add Aliases*

When you send mail regularly to a person who has a hard-to-remember or long e-mail address, you can have ELM define an alias for the user's true e-mail address. For example, you might designate an alias of "Jim" for jrice@stpaul. msr.hp.com. An alias should be much easier to remember and to type than someone's full e-mail address. You can add aliases by using the Alias submenu in the ELM interface.

```
┌─                                Mail                              ─ ┌─┐
│      Mailbox is '/usr/mail/jrice' with 4 message(s) [Elm revision: 70.85]
│
│         1    May 2   root@home.stpaul.m (16)    A short note about Mondays
│         2    May 2   root@home.stpaul.m (14)    Mail Test
│     N   3    May 2   Bill Bigelow         (11)    Calendar Items for next week
│     N   4    May 2   Jim Rice             (11)    Reminder for June Deadlines
│
│
│
│
│
│                           Alias commands
│
│      A)lias current msg,  M)ake new alias,  D)elete alias  or  Check a P)erson.
│          E)xpand and check alias,  List  U)ser  or  S)ystem aliases.
│
│  Alias: █
│
│
├──────────────────────────────────────────────────────────────────┤
│  Alias   Make    Delete   Check      Mail     Expanded Display Display Return
│ Current   Alias    Alias    Person               Address  User    System  to Main
```

The ELM Interface Alias menu.

In this submenu you can make or delete aliases for any person or group of people you send mail to. You can list the aliases that you have compiled for your personal use, or list the aliases that your system administrator may have furnished.

5

Customizing the HP VUE Environment

Regardless of how you use your workstation, what applications you run, or how many hours a day you spend at your keyboard, it's important that the look and feel of your desktop environment fit the way you like to work. You may decide that you don't like the colors on your desktop. Or, maybe the look of the backdrop behind your windows doesn't fit your tastes. Maybe you like to hear the keyboard click as you type. How to make these changes to your HP VUE desktop environment is described in this chapter.

The HP VUE Style Manager

Front Panel Icon

You can begin using the HP VUE Style Manager by selecting the graphic that looks like a small collection of tools and workspace elements on the HP VUE Front Panel. Select the icon by moving the mouse pointer over the graphic and pressing the left mouse button once.

HP VUE Environment

The icon used to start the HP VUE Style Manager.

Once you've selected the HP VUE Style Manager icon, the Style Manager window opens to display icons that invoke the various tools you'll use to configure the look and feel of the HP VUE environment.

The HP VUE Style Manager window.

The HP Style Manager presents nine different tools that are used to customize your desktop environment. The Style Manager's tools include applications to customize

    O   The desktop's colors

    O   The fonts used by your applications

    O   The graphic backdrops for your workspaces

    O   The keyboard behavior

○ The mouse characteristics

○ The beep tone

○ The screen saver

○ The behavior of the windows

○ The start-up (and log out) behavior of HP VUE

Each of these tools can be invoked from the Style Manager window by using the mouse to point at the graphic for the desired tool and selecting it with a single click of the left mouse button. The following sections cover each of these tools in detail.

The HP Style Manager Color Selection Dialog

Style Manager ➡ *Color* ➡

The colors that are used in your desktop environment can be selected using the Color tool found in the HP Style Manager. Colors within the HP VUE environment come in collections called "palettes." A palette is a named collection of colors that, most of the time, complement each other when used in an application. HP VUE comes with a large number of predefined palettes that can be used. The available palettes can be viewed in the scroll box found on the upper part of the Style Manager's Color tool.

The HP Style Manager Color dialog box.

If you want to define your own color palette, you can use the Add... button next to the list of currently available palettes. Pressing the Add... button displays a dialog box that allows you to set up your new personal style.

If you decide to remove a palette from your color palette list, you may delete the one currently selected by pressing the Delete... button found next to the list of available palettes. You will be asked to confirm your deletion of the selected color palette.

Of course, a palette may be close to your ideal color combination, but contain one or two color cells that aren't to your liking. Maybe that mustard yellow cell would suit you better with more green in it. Or maybe, the brown cell has a little too much red for your taste. You can change the color of an individual color cell in a palette by clicking on the cell you'd like to change and then selecting the Modify... button on the Style Manager's Color dialog.

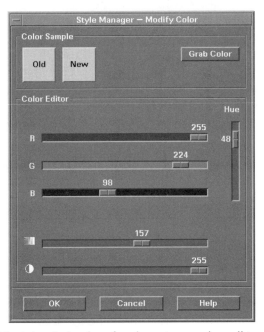

The Modify Color dialog box for changing a color cell in a palette.

After pressing the Modify... button, you'll see a dialog appear that allows you to change the individual red, green, or blue values of your chosen cell. This dialog will display the new and old values for the color cell, and a variety of controls for setting the new color value.

In general, you should adjust the intensities of the red, green, and blue components for your new color cell. Since all colors on your workstation's display are made up of these three basic colors, the trick is in determining how much of each you need to mix to build your new color. You can either change these values explicitly by using the red, green, and blue sliders, by changing the hue and intensity sliders located next to the red, green, and blue sliders, or by pressing the Grab Color button. The Grab Color button will change your cursor to a small cross hair. Use the cross hair to point and click to "grab a color" from anyplace on your display. The color you select will be assigned to the color cell you are changing.

Once your color cell looks the way you want, you can select the OK button found at the bottom of the Modify Color dialog.

If you don't like your color changes, you can cancel any that you made to the cell by selecting the Cancel button.

Finally, as with most HP VUE dialog boxes, if you have any questions about how to use the dialog, you can always select the Help button.

We've spent lots of time talking about how to select a color palette and how to change an individual cell in that color palette, but how do you know how many cells will be available in any given palette? Well, you can decide how many available cells you want by selecting the Color Use button on the HP VUE Style Manager Color dialog.

Choosing the Color Use... button displays a dialog that allows you to choose between the various levels of color used by the HP VUE Window Manager. The Window Manager can use a large number of colors if left to its own devices. If you are using applications that need a large number of colors themselves—mechanical design, image processing, or page layout—you could run into a situation where HP VUE doesn't leave you enough colors for your "real" work. You can avoid this situation by reducing the number of colors that HP VUE can use through the Style Manager's Color Use dialog.

A dialog box that sets the number of colors used by HP VUE.

Through the HP VUE Color Use dialog, you can choose between High Color, Medium Color, Low Color, Mono-chrome, and the Default for your display controller. The High Color option is used for displays that have a large number of color cells available to them, such as the common eight plane systems, which offer 256 or more colors. The Mono-chrome option uses the least number of colors by restricting HP VUE to only the built-in black and white colors. (Please, I don't want to get calls reminding me that black isn't really a color.)

The High Color option sets aside enough colors to support eight color cells for the current HP VUE color palette. If this is too many colors for your applications, you can choose the Medium, Low, or Monochrome levels. The Medium level will set aside colors for four cells. The Low level will set aside colors for two color cells. Finally, the Monochrome level will restrict HP VUE to using only black and white for its display graphics.

HP VUE Environment

The HP Style Manager Font Dialog

Style Manager ➡ *Font*

Not all users like to see the same size fonts in all of their applications. Users of HP VUE are no exception. The Style Manager offers a tool that makes it easy to change your system's default font size for the HP VUE environment and applications that run within the HP VUE environment.

Invoke the Font dialog box by selecting the Font icon on the HP VUE Style Manager window. A window opens that you use to select the default font size for your environment. This window consists of two main work areas: the Size selection area and the font Preview area.

The HP VUE Font Selection Tool.

After opening the Font tool, you can select the size of the default font from the options displayed in the Size work area.

These options may range from fonts smaller than most humans can comfortably read to fonts that make your applications take up most of the display. Use the scroll bar in this work area to view all font sizes that are available to you.

After selecting the size of the font, the Preview area will immediately update to display a sample of the font that you've selected. The Preview area has two basic fields. The upper field displays a known sample of the selected font, made up of a mix of numeric and alphabetic characters used by the system. The lower field offers an editable area in which you can type your own text, to make sure that the size you've selected is acceptable.

 NOTE: Changes that you make to the default font size won't take effect until an application is started (or restarted). This means that, for example, terminal windows already on your display will remain unaffected. However, new terminal windows will reflect your new font selection.

Selecting the HP VUE Workspace Backdrop Graphics

Style Manager ➡ *Backdrop*

One of the really attractive features of the HP VUE environment is the number of workspaces available to help you organize your windows into logical collections. When switching between these workspaces, one thing that helps you differentiate between them is the graphics that are visible on the background of the workspaces. In order to set or change

HP VUE Environment

these graphics, the HP VUE Style Manager offers a Backdrop tool. Invoke this tool by pointing at the Backdrop icon on the Style Manager window and selecting it.

The HP VUE Style Manager Backdrop dialog.

Once you select the Backdrop icon, a dialog box opens on your desktop, displaying two basic work areas. The graphic preview area is on the left side. A scrolling area on the right allows you to select the backdrop you want to use.

To change the backdrop graphic in your current window, use the scroll bar and mouse to locate the graphic that you'd like on your background. Once you locate the name of the graphic, you can preview it by selecting it within the scrolling list area. Highlighting the graphic name displays the graphic in the preview window (or part of the graphic if it's too big to fit in the preview window). You can assign the graphic to the backdrop of your current workspace by pressing OK at the bottom of the dialog.

As always, two other buttons exist next to the OK button on the bottom of the dialog: Cancel and Help. You can cancel the backdrop dialog, before you make any changes to the workspace background, by pressing the Cancel button. Or, if you want more help about backdrops, workspaces, or using the backdrop dialog, you can press the Help button.

Selecting the Keyboard Behavior for HP VUE

Style Manager ➡ *Keyboard*

Many people have a very definite idea about how their keyboards should feel and sound. To accommodate these people, the HP VUE Style Manager includes a tool that can modify some of your keyboard's behavior. You can open the keyboard dialog by selecting the Keyboard icon on the HP VUE Style Manager window.

The HP VUE Style Manager Keyboard dialog.

Use the HP VUE Style Manager Keyboard dialog to turn Auto Repeat on and off and to set the Click Volume. Auto Repeat may happen if you press and hold any key on the keyboard. After a short delay, the key that is pressed will be rapidly repeated until you let up on the key. Click Volume controls the "click" sound that the computer makes whenever you

HP VUE Environment

press a key on the keyboard. The audio hardware in your computer makes this sound, and it comes out of the audio speaker.

> ⊜ *NOTE: You can turn the keyboard click off by setting the Click Volume to zero.*

> ⊜ *NOTE: There are special keys on your keyboard called modifier keys that change the behavior of the other keys on your keyboard. These special keys include the <Shift> key and the <Ctrl> key. Modifier keys are not affected when Auto Repeat or keyboard clicks are enabled.*

Selecting the Mouse Behavior for HP VUE

Style Manager ➡ Mouse

A user's mouse behavior is important. Not only is a user accustomed to a mouse that works a certain way, it's also necessary that the mouse be able to operate in the amount of desk space that's available for it. Aside from how the mouse moves across the desktop, how the buttons behave is important as well. Is the user left-handed or right-handed? Is the user an old mouse hand, or brand new to the world of mice? The HP VUE Style Manager's Mouse dialog can configure the mouse to accommodate the different mouse behavior that people require. Open the Mouse dialog by selecting the Mouse icon on the HP VUE Style Manager window.

The HP VUE Style Manager Mouse dialog allows the user to adjust both the mouse's button behavior, and how the cursor on the display tracks with the mouse as it moves across the desk next to your keyboard. First we'll talk about the button behavior and then we'll describe how to adjust the pointer tracking.

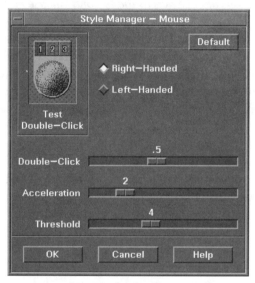

The HP VUE Style Manager Mouse dialog.

The mouse, sitting next to your keyboard, typically has three buttons near its leading edge. These buttons are generally numbered 1, 2 and 3 from left to right. This arrangement works well if you are right-handed because it places the first mouse button, the Select button, conveniently under your index finger. However, if you are left-handed, this arrangement can be pretty awkward. For this reason, the Mouse dialog allows you to reverse the order of the buttons on the mouse from 1, 2, 3 to 3, 2, 1, making the arrangement of the buttons more convenient for left-handed mouse users.

HP VUE Environment

> ✏️ *NOTE:* *Some very old mice on HP workstations may only have two buttons. If you have one of these mice you should probably think about getting a new one. In the meantime, HP VUE will simulate a three-button mouse by using the two buttons as one and three. Pressing both buttons at once acts as the "second" mouse button.*

Now that you've figured out which mouse button is which, you need to figure out how fast you need to click the mouse button to accomplish a double-click. A double-click is two consecutive clicks of the mouse button with a very small time interval in between. You can configure this time interval using the top slider on the dialog.

If you are used to manipulating a mouse and clicking madly away in your applications, you can probably set this interval to be very small. If you are new to mousing around, or just have a laid back mousing style, you might want to set the time interval to be a little longer.

The last two sliders on the Mouse dialog set the Accelerate and Threshold values for your mouse. These two values control how fast and how far the cursor on the display moves as you move the mouse device around on your desk. The more experienced you are with a mouse and the smaller the space you have allocated on your desk for the mouse, the higher you'll want to set these values. However, you should set these carefully. If they are too high, your cursor will seem to jump all the way across the screen at the slightest touch of the mouse. This can make it difficult to get any work done at all.

If, in your attempt to get the mouse set up perfectly, you find that you've made the mouse almost unusable (I've been known to do this myself a few times), see if you can get the cursor back over the default button on the dialog. Pressing on this button will return the mouse attributes to their factory defaults.

If you've managed to get the mouse tuned to your liking, press the OK button to close the Mouse dialog. If not, you can press the Cancel button to close the dialog without making any changes at all. If you want more details on how to use the Mouse dialog, or just want to understand more about customizing the mouse behavior, press the Help button. All of these buttons can be found along the bottom of the Mouse dialog window.

Setting the Tone for HP VUE

Style Manager ➡ *Beeper*

Periodically, HP VUE—and applications running under HP VUE—need to alert you that something special has happened, usually by making some type of short beeper sound. The pitch, duration, and volume of the beep sound can be customized using the HP VUE Style Manager Beeper dialog. Open the Beeper dialog by using the mouse to select the Beeper icon on the HP VUE Style Manager window.

The Beeper dialog contains three sliders that you can use to adjust the Volume, Tone, and Duration of the beeper used by the HP VUE environment. You can move each of these sliders by pointing at it with the cursor and pressing and holding the left mouse button as you move the slider where you want it. Moving the Volume slider to the right increases the volume of the beeper tone. Moving the Tone slider to the right increases the pitch of the beeper tone (possibly driving dogs to distraction if you move it too far). The last slider increases the length of time that the beeper tone is sounded.

The HP VUE Style Manager Beeper dialog.

Once you've chosen comfortable values for the Volume, Tone, and Duration, you can press the OK button to close the Beeper dialog. If you've modified the tone and would like to return it to its original values, press the Default button.

The Cancel and Help buttons are self-explanatory. If you've made some changes that you don't want to save, press the Cancel button. If you'd like to get more help or information about setting the beeper tone, you can always press the Help button. (Real technocrats never read the directions or press the Help buttons. The rest of us use them quite a bit.)

Setting the Screen Saver Behavior for HP VUE

Style Manager ➡ *Screens*

Whether for improving the security of your information or simply to keep from burning a ghost into your display, an important feature of your computer is its screen saver. You can configure the screen saver for your computer by using a Screen dialog available in the HP VUE Style Manager. Invoke this dialog by selecting the Screen icon from the HP VUE Style Manager window.

The Screen dialog box allows you to configure two aspects of the screen display: the screen saver and the screen lock. The screen saver is a facility of the HP VUE Window Manager that will blank your display (that is, turn it off) when nothing is happening with your keyboard or mouse. The screen lock facility protects your display from unauthorized use. When your display is locked, you must type your password, or the password of the superuser, to gain access to any of the applications or windows that are running on your display.

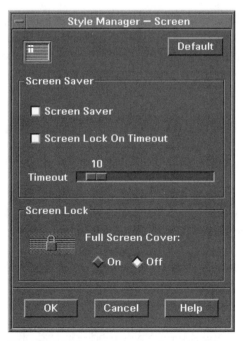

The HP VUE Style Manager Screen dialog.

The top toggle button on the Screen dialog box determines if the HP VUE screen saver is active. If it's depressed, the screen saver will blank the screen when there has been no keyboard or mouse activity for a short period of time. You can configure the amount of idle time with the slider found at the bottom of the upper pane. As you move the slider to the right, the amount of time that the keyboard and mouse must be idle before the screen is blanked increases. The amount of time in minutes will be displayed above the slider as it is moved.

Optionally, you may wish to have the display locked at the same time that it is blanked. You can enable this feature of the screen saver by depressing the Screen Lock on Timeout toggle button, located just below the Screen Saver toggle button.

When the Screen Lock is activated (either by toggling on the Screen Lock on Timeout feature or by pressing the padlock found on the bottom of the Front Panel), it has two possible modes of operation. These modes are Full Screen Cover on or off.

If the Full Screen Cover is on, when the screen locks, the screen will be covered by a solid color window that will obscure all the applications running on your display. This will protect your applications from prying eyes.

When the screen is locked with the Full Screen Cover off, keyboard inputs will be ignored just as when the screen cover is on. Only now, all of the application windows are visible. This is a handy way to protect your applications from accidental interruption while leaving them available for someone to monitor.

You can turn the screen cover mode on and off by selecting the radio button on the bottom of the Screen dialog box.

Once you've selected the Screen Saver and Screen Lock behavior, you can press the OK button to accept the changes and close the Screen dialog. Alternately, you can press the Cancel button to close the dialog and cancel any changes you may have made.

You may also get additional help by pressing the Help dialog button. The Help button produces a window providing additional information about the Screen Saver, Screen Locks, timeouts, and so on.

Looking at Windows in HP VUE

Style Manager ➥ *Window*

As you work with windows on your desktop, you have to decide how you'd like them to react to your mouse pointer, what you'd like to see as you move the windows, and where you want them placed when you iconify them. The HP VUE Style Manager provides a dialog for customizing these aspects of the windows. To open the Window dialog, use the mouse to select the Window icon on the HP VUE Style Manager window.

The first configuration option on the Window dialog is the window focus resource for the HP VUE Window Manager. The window focus resource determines how you select a window on your desktop to receive the input from keyboard and mouse. While all application windows on your desktop remain active, only one window at a time can receive input from the mouse and keyboard. The window that receives this input is referred to as the window that's in focus.

HP VUE Environment

The HP VUE Style Manager Window dialog.

The HP VUE Window Manager can focus on a window in two ways: as soon as the mouse pointer crosses onto it, or when the window is selected using the mouse pointer explicitly. You can select how to have the window come into focus by choosing one of the top two radio buttons on the Window dialog.

Once you've decided which way you'd like to have the windows come into focus, you need to decide if you want the window raised to the top when it comes into focus. You can choose to have the window rise on top of all the windows that might be obscuring it by depressing the Raise with Focus button on the dialog.

The next item to configure is how the window appears while it's being moved around on the display. (You move a window by pressing and holding the left mouse button on the title bar of a window and dragging it to a new place on the display.) You have two choices of what you see as you move the window to its new location. The default is a box outline that represents the moving window. This window outline will be replaced by the window itself when you release the mouse button.

Alternately, you can drag the window itself to its new location. Moving the window itself is referred to as an "opaque move." An opaque move requires a much faster X window server than an outline move. You can choose opaque moves by depressing the button on the Window dialog labeled "Opaque Move."

The final thing you can configure using the Window dialog is where window icons are placed on the display—either in an icon box or right on the desktop. An icon box is a special window in which all HP VUE Window Manager icons can be placed. Configure the icon placement by choosing one of the radio buttons located in the bottom pane of the dialog.

Once you've decided how you want your windows to behave, press the OK button to close the window. If you want to cancel any changes, press the Cancel button before you close the window. If you want to learn more about configuring your window resources, you can choose the Help button.

HP VUE Environment

Startup and Log Out Behavior for HP VUE

Style Manager ➡ *Startup*

Every time you log onto your workstation, you begin what's referred to as a "session." Your session consists of the applications that are running on your display. The HP VUE Window Manager allows you to configure which applications will be running on your workstation when you log in by using the the Startup dialog. You can open this dialog by pointing at the Startup icon, on the HP VUE Style Manager, and pressing the left mouse button.

The HP VUE Style Manager Startup dialog box.

You have two basic options for defining the applications that are running when you log in. You can instruct HP VUE to try to determine which applications are running when you log out. It will then try to restart these applications the next time you log in.

Instead of trying to restart the applications that existed at logout, you can have the HP VUE Window Manager start a Home Session. A Home Session is a well-defined collection of applications. You can configure your Home Session by starting and arranging the applications that you want to use at startup and then pressing the Set Home Session... button.

If you don't want to decide immediately what you'd like to see at startup, when you log out you can instruct the Window Manager to ask you at the next login what you'd like to see.

The final thing you need to decide is if you want HP VUE to ask you to confirm your logout request. If you choose to have your logout request confirmed, you will be presented with a logout confirmation window before you end your current session.

After you decide how you'd like your session to start and stop, you can close the Startup dialog by pressing the OK button. Press the Cancel button to cancel any changes that you may have made. Additional help on sessions, home environments, and more can be found by pressing the Help button.

6

101 Commonly Used UNIX Commands

This chapter covers 101 of the most commonly used UNIX commands supported by the HP-UX operating environment.

adjust

```
adjust [-bcjr] [-m column] [-t tabsize]
files...
```

This command is a simple text formatting utility.

Switches and Options:

-b	Don't convert leading blanks to tabs; replace tabs with blank spaces.
-c	Centers text on the lines.
-j	Justifies the paragraphs by filling lines (except the last line of the paragraph) with spaces.
-r	Right justifies the text.
-m column	Sets the right margin to *column* instead of the default 72.
-t tabsize	Changes the tab size from the default eight to *tabsize*.

alias

```
alias [-x] [alias_name]=commands
```

This command allows you to define shortcut replacements for HP-UX commands. For instance,

```
$    alias dir=ls
```

helps a user accustomed to the DOS environment by mapping a common DOS command to its UNIX equivalent.

Switches and Options:

-x   Lists or displays an exported alias. An exported alias is one that remains in effect for all subshells of the present shell.

Remarks and Cautions:

A command that takes arguments or options must be set in single or double quotes. Make sure the open and close quotes match. For instance,

```
$    alias promptcd="export PS1='pwd';cd"
```

allows the alias promptcd to change the current shell prompt to show what the new working directory is.

The alias command is a feature of the shell that you are using. The alias command described here is defined by the Korn shell (/bin/ksh). The behavior of the alias command may vary, depending on the shell you are using.

Other Uses and Suggestions:

alias by itself will display a list of all aliases currently in effect.

alias alias_name will display the definition for alias_name.

at

```
at [-m][-f filename][-q queue] time
[date] [[next | +increment]
time_designation] job ...

at -r job ...

at -l job ...
```

This command runs a specified command or program at some specified future time. For example,

```
$   at -f backup.at 0200 ↵
```

would run a backup script at 2 AM. The backup script would include necessary tar, cpio, fbackup, or nbsbackup lines to back up selected files and directories to tape; an optional at -f backup.at 0200 as the last line in the script would reinvoke the at command for the following day.

> 📇 **NOTE:** *The .at suffix is not required, but does make it easier to identify the file in a directory list.*

Switches and Options:

time
: May be entered as a one, two, or four digit number representing the hour and/ or minutes of the day. Alternately, the hours and minutes may be separated by a colon, a period, a single quote, or a comma. The special keywords noon, midnight, now, or next may also be used.

✔ **TIP:** Additional keywords and separators are available through the use of HP-UX native language support. For more information, refer to langinfo.

date
: Schedules the job for the specified date. Without a specified date argument, at will run the job when the specified time (see previous option) comes around again.

-f *filename*	Using the -f switch followed by a filename causes at to get the commands for the job it is to schedule from the filename indicated after the switch.
-r	Removes the specified job(s) from the queue. You can use the -l switch to get a listing of current jobs in the queue.
-l	Displays a list of pending at jobs, including their job numbers. If no jobs are pending, it merely returns to the shell's prompt.
-m	Causes at to send mail to the user submitting the job when it has finished. The mail will include all standard and error output produced by the job.
-q *queue*	Submits the job to specified queue instead of to default queue a. Queues a, b, and d through y, are the available queues.

Remarks and Cautions:

This command does not act on aliases. You must use an actual command name. Two files govern permissions for job submission: /usr/lib/cron/at.allow and /usr/lib/cron/at.deny.

If at.deny exists and is empty, then global job submission permission is granted. If any *user_names* exist in at.deny, your *user_name* must appear in at.allow. Otherwise, only a superuser may submit jobs.

See also: batch, cron, crontab

basename

```
basename string [suffix]
```

This command removes the directory pathname and the suffix, if provided, from the pathname provided. The result is the simple leaf name of the file; for example,

```
$    basename /users/jrice/myfile.txt .txt↵
     myfile
```

See also: dirname

batch

batch *script* | *command*

The batch command schedules a job for execution as soon as the system load level permits. It is functionally equivalent to at -q b *now*. For instance,

$ batch newjob⏎

immediately executes the script newjob when the system load level permits.

Switches and Options:

The batch command has no switches.

See also: at

bdf

```
bdf [-b] [-i] [-l|-L] [-t type] |
Filesystem | file ... ]
```

This command reports the amount of available and free disk space on the filesystems available to your computer.

Keying bdf by itself displays usage statistics for all filesystems currently mounted on your computer.

Categories are as follows:

O **Filesystem**: the name of the filesystems.

O **kbytes**: the total number of 1024-byte blocks on the device.

O **used**: the total number of 1024-byte blocks used on the device.

O **avail**: the number of 1024-byte blocks available to be used on the device.

O **capacity**: the percentage of the device that is being used for storage.

O **mounted on:** the location in your filesystem where the device is mounted.

Switches and Options:

-b	Displays information about filesystem swapping.
-i	Lists the number of free and used i-nodes on the filesystems.
-l	In an HP cluster environment, displays information about the filesystems mounted on the local c-node.

-L   In an HP cluster environment, displays in-
                      formation about the filesystems on the local
                      c-node, which may be unmounted.

-t *type*   Reports information about a specific file-
                      system type such as NFS, HFS, or CDFS.

Remarks and Cautions:

You may notice—if you're being observant—that the available disk space and the used disk space don't add up to the
total amount of disk space on some filesystems. This is
because there is a small amount of disk space that is reserved
by the system and isn't available to typical users. This disk
space is used to improve the efficiency of the disk allocation
mechanisms and to keep the system operational when a user
accidentally (and it is always an accident) fills the disk up.

See also: df

cal

```
cal [[month] year]
```

This command displays a calendar for the specified month and year. For instance,

```
$  cal 4 1994↵
```

displays a calendar for April 1994.

Switches and Options:

Without any arguments, the cal command will accept up to two numeric arguments. These two arguments are the month and year about which you would like the cal command to display information. These arguments can be numbers from 1 to 12 for the month and from 1 to 1999 for the year. If you only provide a single numeric argument, the cal command will assume that it is the year and provide information about all months in that particular year.

Other Uses and Suggestions:

Check out the calendar for September 1752, the month and year that the calendar switched from Gregorian to Julian.

See also: calendar, cron

calendar

```
calendar -
```

This command checks a file named `calendar` in the current directory and displays lines with today's or tomorrow's date. For instance,

```
$    calendar↵

$    Monday, Nov 11th: Group Meeting at 2:00
```

Switches and Options:

-          Nope, it is not a typo. The - argument runs `calendar` for all users on the system. However, this option can only be run by the system administrator. It is typically run out of `cron` early in the morning.

See also: `cron`

cat

```
cat [-su] [-v [-t] [-e]] file ...
```

displays one or more text files on screen. For instance,

```
$   cat myfile
```

would display the file myfile on screen.

```
$   cat -v myfile⏎
```

would display the file named myfile on the screen with nonprinting characters printed visibly.

Switches and Options:

-s	Makes cat silent about nonexistent files.
-u	Display output will not be buffered.
-v	Causes nonprinting characters (except tabs, new-lines, and form-feeds) to print visibly.
-t	When used with the -v, causes all tab characters to be displayed as ^I characters.
-e	When used with the -v, causes all new-line characters to be prefaced with a $ before they are printed.

Remarks and Cautions:

cat by itself accepts input from the keyboard, sending it to the screen when you key an end-of-file character. This command accepts redirection, which permits you to concatenate two or more files and redirect the output to another file, thus creating a new file.

```
$   cat old_file another_old_file appended_
    file
```

See also: more, page, pg

cd

```
cd dir_name
```

This command changes the current working directory. When *dir_name* is specified, you are switched to the named directory. If *dir_name* is not specified, you are switched to your home directory. For instance,

```
$    cd /users/jrice/documents/hpqr↵
```

switches to the directory where I store the text files for this book. If I then key in

```
$    cd
```

I would be returned to my home directory.

chgrp

chgrp [-R] *group filename* ...

This command changes the group ownership for specified files. For instance,

$ chgrp design projects.txt⏎

assigns the file projects.txt to the design group.

Switches and Options:

- R   Causes the chgrp command to change the group ownership of the specified directory, along with all the files and subdirectories, to the group that is specified on the command line.

Remarks and Cautions:

You may only change group ownership of a file or directory if (1) you are the owner of the file, or (2) you are the superuser.

Other Uses and Suggestions:

Use groups to see which groups you are a member of.

---

chmod (Absolute mode)

chmod [-R] *mode filename* ...

This command changes the permissions mode of specified files. Permissions may be set using either absolute or symbolic mode. For instance,

    $ chmod 660 inventory.wk1⏎

is an absolute mode command giving read and write permissions to the owner and the group for the file inventory. wk1.

Absolute Mode Notation

Absolute mode is an octal number based on the following codes:

○ **Other Users**

0004	Read by the world
0002	Write by the world
0001	Execute by the world

○ **Group Members**

0040	Read by the group
0020	Write by the group
0010	Execute by the group

○ **File Owner**

0400	Read by the owner
0200	Write by the owner
0100	Execute by the owner

○ **Special Cases**

4000   Set userid on execution (execute)

2000   Set groupid on execution (ignore if file is a directory)

1000   Set sticky bit (may help this program run faster at the cost of a little extra memory and disk space)

In octal notation, the numbers in each column are additive with the number in the same column of subsequent groups. Therefore, since no one is being given execute permission in the previous example, the first number is 0.

To give the group read and write permission, the second number is 040 + 020 = 060.

The owner has read and write permission, so the third number is 400 + 200 = 600.

If any of the special cases were being assigned, the fourth number would be the octal sum of the fourth column numbers. In the example, if all three user categories were given read, write previous, and execute permission on the file, the mode would be 777.

✏️ *NOTE: Leading zeros may be omitted. In the previous example, none of the special cases are assigned to the file.*

Switches and Options:

-R   Causes chmod to operate on the specified directory and any subdirectories or files that may exist.

See also: chgrp, chown, groups, ls

chmod (Symbolic mode)

```
chmod [-A] [-R] [who]
operation [permission] [,...]
filename
```

In symbolic mode, chmod uses symbolic rather than octal notation to set file modes. For instance,

```
$    chmod a +x inventory.wk1↵
```

gives execute permission to all users for the file inventory.wk1.

The *who* variable is a combination of the following:

u	user
g	group
o	other
a	all

The *operation* variable can be

+	Adds permission
-	Removes permission
=	Explicitly assigns a permission while resetting the others
X	Gives execute permission for a directory
s	Sets ownerid or groupid
t	Sets sticky bit

The *permission* variable can be

r	Read
w	Write
x	Execute

Switches and Options:

- A   Preserves any access control lists assigned
               to the file. Access control lists are a special
               type of control that may be placed on the
               files of some filesystems.

- R   Causes chmod to operate on the specified
               directory and any files or subdirectories that
               might exist.

See also: chacl, chgrp, chown, groups, ls

chown

chown [-R] *owner filename(s)*

This command changes a file's owner. The owner may be either *user_name* or *userid*. For instance,

$ chown -R billb holidays⏎

would change ownership of the file holidays to user billb. It would do so recursively for all files of that name in subsequent subdirectories.

Switches and Options:

-R   Causes chown to operate on the specified directory and any files or subdirectories that might exist.

Remarks and Cautions:

Only a superuser can change ownership. When a symbolic link is encountered, ownership is changed only for the specified file; the link is not traversed.

See also: chgrp, chmod, groups, ls

clear

```
clear
```

This command clears the screen or shell window and places the cursor in the upper left corner.

```
$   clear⏎
```

Remarks and Cautions:

If clear appears not to work, use set to check the term variable. Set it to a valid terminal type. For instance, the following line in your .profile will make the terminal do some checking and set itself.

```
TERM='tset -Q -'; export TERM
```

> **NOTE:** *Key in the line exactly per the example, with the matching quotes, the capital Q, and the lone dash.*

> **NOTE:** *This example works fine for the Bourne, Korn, and Posix shells. Other shells may have a slightly different syntax.*

cmp

cmp [-i] [-s] *file1 file2*

This command compares two files and reports the byte location and line number if they are different.

Switches and Options:

-1   Prints the byte number and the octal value of the differing byte if the two files are different.

-s   Causes cmp to remain silent and exit with a non-zero status if the two files are different.

See also: diff

col

```
col [-blfxp]
```

This command is a simple text filter used to process line-feeds and backspaces in formatted files.

Switches and Options:

-b	Processes the file for an output device that doesn't support backspaces.
-l	Processes the file for a line printer device that supports over-strikes.
-f	Allows the output file to include half-line (fine) advancements.
-x	Allows the output file to contain blank spaces and doesn't replace them with tabs.
-p	Causes col to pass control characters rather than ignore them in the input. (This can cause some pretty messy output.)

☞ **NOTE:** *This command is used frequently to filter man pages for reading as a plain text file. For example,*

```
$ man col |col -b col.man↵
```

produces a text file named col.man that doesn't contain any of the formatting characters for your local display. It can be viewed and edited in any text editor without all the extra control characters.

compress

```
compress [-d] [-f] [-v] [-c] [-V]
[-b maxbits] filename ...
```

This command compresses files to conserve space on the storage media. The result of the compress command is an output file with a filename the same as the input file with a .Z appended to the end. For instance,

```
$   compress -v myfile.text↵
```

would compress myfile.text, replacing the input file with a file named myfile.text.Z. It would then display the percent by which the original file was compressed.

Switches and Options:

-d   Decompresses the *filename*. This is the same as uncompress *filename*.

-f   Forces compression, even if *compressed_filename* exists. It also causes compress to produce a "compressed file," even if the resulting file is larger than the original.

-v   Displays percentage of compression possible. This switch leaves the specified file unchanged and doesn't result in a compressed output file.

-c   Reports the result of the compress (or uncompress) to the display. The command compress -d -c *filename* is the same as zcat *filename*.

-V   Displays the current version and compiles options onto the standard error stream of the display.

-b *maxbits*   Specifies the number of bits the compress algorithm uses. The default is 16. The valid range is between 9 and 16 bits.

Remarks and Cautions:

`compress` replaces the source file. The new file has the same name as the source, with a .Z extension. If file cannot be made smaller by compression, `compress` will return having done nothing to the input file.

See also: `uncompress, zcat`

cp

```
cp [-f|-i] [-p] source_name
target_pathname

cp [-f|-i] [-p] file1 [file2 ...]
dest_directory

cp [-f|-i] [-p] -R|-r directory1
[directory2 ...] dest_directory
```

This command copies one or more files, or a directory, leaving the original in place. For instance,

```
$   cp -i myfile $HOME/hold↵
```

would create a copy of myfile in the hold directory, which is a subdirectory of your home directory. It would prompt for confirmation if a file by the same name already exists.

⊟▷ *NOTE: Using $HOME saves some typing if the absolute path to your home directory is long.*

⊟▷ *NOTE: All directory names in the pathname for the destination must exist or the copy will fail.*

Switches and Options:

-f	Forces the removal of destination pathnames that might already exist with the same name as the destination.
-i	Prompts for confirmation if cp will overwrite an existing file. Otherwise, overwrite occurs without warning.
-p	Copies the file or directory, including modification time and permissions.
-r	If any of the source files are subdirectories, the subdirectories and their files will be copied also; the target must also be a directory.

-R This switch is the same as -r except that new directories are copied with read, write, and search permission for the owner. Group and world permissions are kept the same as the source tree.

Remarks and Cautions:

By default, if *target_file* exists, its mode and owner will be preserved; otherwise, the mode and owner of *source_file* will be assigned.

If *source_name* is a symbolic link, cp copies the actual file, but not the link. cp accepts wildcards. For instance,

```
$   cp -i my* /hold
```

would copy all files in the current working directory that begin with "my," and would prompt for confirmation if any files already exist in /hold.

If the last entry in the target pathname is a valid subdirectory, cp creates a copy of the source file in that subdirectory. Otherwise, it creates a new file, using the last field of the pathname as the new filename, placing the copy in the existing directory. The target directory must exist for cp to function.

☞ *WARNING: Be careful of the -r switch. Recursively copying a subdirectory to a subdirectory of itself will continue copying until the filesystem is full.*

See also: cpio, ln, mv, tar

cpio

This command is used to create or read file archives, copying them to or from tape or disk. It can also be used to copy files from one directory to another. Filenames to copy or restore are taken from the standard input.

    cpio -o [-aABcxvCh]

    cpio -i [BdcrtuxvmfPsSb6Ru] [patterns]

    cpio -p [aduxvlmrU] directory

This command takes three basic forms. cpio -o is used to create a backup image of a list of filenames that are provided to it through its standard input. cpio -i is used to restore a backup image to your filesystem. Finally, cpio -p is used to move a file or directory to another location in your filesystem. For instance,

    $ find /users/jrice -print |cpio -o
         /dev/rmt/0m

writes all the files in the /users/jrice/tree to a tape archive.

    $ cpio -idmv /dev/rmt/0m

restores all files from a tape archive.

    $ find. -print |cpio -pdmvu
         $HOME/copy.tree

moves a copy of everything from the local directory to a subdirectory of my home directory called copy.tree.

Switches and Options:

    -a   Resets access times of files as they are
                copied.

    -A   Suppresses warning messages.

-B	Blocks input/output into 5,120 bytes per record. This is only applies to data being written to devices that support variable length records such as tape drives.
-d	Creates subdirectories, if required.
-c	Reads or write headers in ASCII form.
-r	Renames files interactively. If you press the <Enter> key without entering a new filename, then the file is skipped.
-t	Prints a table of contents of the input archive.
-u	Unconditionally copies.
-x	Saves or restores device special files, such as those in the /dev directory.
-v	Causes a verbose process.
-l	Wherever possible, links files rather than copies them. (Only applicable when used with the -p option.)
-m	Retains previous modification times.
-f	Copies in files except those in the supplied pattern.
-p	Reads a file written on a PDP-11 or VAX system (these systems require that the bytes be swapped around) if the tape wasn't written using the -c option.
-s	Swaps all the bytes of the file.
-S	Swaps all the half words around.
-b	Swaps both the half words and the bytes around.
-6	Processes a UNIX sixth-edition format file.
-R	Resynchronizes automatically when cpio goes "out of phase."

-C   Has cpio checkpoint itself at the start of
                    each volume.

-h   Operates on the files that symbolic links
                    point at, rather than on the links themselves.

-U   Uses the systems file-mode creation mask
                    (umask) to set the mode of the files that are
                    created.

See also: find, tar

cron

cron is a system daemon that executes processes at specific times. Each user who is permitted to schedule automatic processes has a crontab file in /usr/spool/cron/ crontabs.

See also: at, crontab

crontab

```
crontab filename

crontab [-r]

crontab [-1]
```

This command is used to list, install, or remove a user's crontab file. For instance,

```
$   crontab -1
```

would display the crontab belonging to you.

Switches and Options:

-1   Displays your crontab file.

-r   Removes your crontab file from /usr/spool/cron/crontabs.

Remarks and Cautions:

crontab uses the following files:

```
/usr/lib/cron/cron.allow

/usr/lib/cron/cron.deny
```

If neither file exists, only a superuser or root may edit crontab files. Each cron process is scheduled using a separate line in your crontab file. Lines in the crontab file must be entered in the following format. (Each field is separated by a space.)

```
mm hh dd MM DD cmd arguments
```

○ *mm* – minutes past the hour (0–59)

○ *hh* – hour, in 24-hour format (0–23)

○ *dd* – date (1–31)

○ *MM* – month (1–12)

○ *DD* – day of the week (Sun=0, Sat=6)

○ *cmd* – command to run, including complete pathname

○ *additional* – any arguments, such as output redirection. For example, `0 2 * * 1,2,3,4,5 $HOME/backup.script $HOME/backup.log`

At 2 AM, Monday through Friday, `cron` would execute your `backup.script` command, with any output directed to a log file.

⬛▷ *NOTE: Asterisks are used as place-keepers for unused fields. Commas separate multiple entries in a field.*

See also: `at, cron`

---
crypt
---

crypt *password*

This command uses a password to encrypt information. It takes the information from the standard input, encrypts (or decrypts) it, then writes the result to standard output. For instance,

$ crypt noseeum ydata mydata.crypt

crypt also performs the decryption process by reading in the encrypted data and writing the decrypted data to standard output.

$ crypt noseeum ydata.cryptmydata

▷ **NOTE:** *If no password is given to* crypt, *it will stop the encryption/decryption process long enough to prompt the user for the password.*

cut

```
cut [-c] list file ...

cut [-f] list [-d char] [-s] file ...
```

This command can be used to extract, or cut, a column or field from a text file.

Switches and Options:

list	A comma separated list of integer field numbers, such as 1,3,6,7-9;3-7;1,3,5,7
-c list	Extracts the list from the file, interpreting the list as character positions.
-f	Extracts the list from the file, interpreting the list as fields in the file.
-d char	Defines the field delimiter to be char instead of the default tab.
-s	Doesn't process lines that do not contain a delimiter character.

See also: paste

---

date

```
date [-u]

date [-u] +format

date [-u] mmddhhmm[yy]
```

This command allows the systems administrator to set the system time and date and allows you to see it in the standard (no formats used) or in an arbitrary format, using the format directives. For instance,

```
$   date
```

would reveal

Tue Oct 8 11:20:53 CST 1994

If you are the superuser, you can use `date` to set the date and time on your system by entering the following `date` command. For example:

```
$   date 0904170093
```

Switches and Options:

The following options may be used to modify your date display:

%a	Abbreviated weekday name
%A	Full weekday name
%b	Abbreviated month name
%B	Full month name
%c	Current date and time representation
%d	Day of the month as a decimal number (01,31)
%D	Date in usual US format (%m/%d/%y)

%E	Combined Emperor/Era name and year (a blank space on every system I've ever seen it supported on)
%F	Full month name
%h	Abbreviated month name
%H	Hour (24-hour clock) as a decimal number (00,23)
%I	Hour (12-hour clock) as a decimal number (01,12)
%j	Day of the year as a decimal number (001,366)
%m	Month as a decimal number (01,12)
%M	Minute as a decimal number (00,59)
%n	New-line character
%N	Emperor/Era name
%o	Emperor/Era number
%p	Equivalent of AM or PM
%r	Time in 12-hour US format
%S	Second as a decimal number (00,53)
%t	Tab character
%T	Time in 24-hour US format
%U	Week number of the year as a decimal number (00,53) - Sunday as the first day of the week
%w	Weekday as a decimal number (0[Sunday],6)
%W	Week number of the year as a decimal number (00,53) - Monday as the first day of the week
%x	Current date representation
%X	Current time representation

%y	Year without century as a decimal number (00,99)
%Y	Year with century as a decimal number
%Z	Time zone name
%z	Time zone name
%%	%
[-|0]w	An optional spacing (or width) w may follow any % directive. This number defines the minimum number of characters that the directive will use. If the width is preceded by a "-" the data will be left justified in the space defined. If the width is preceded by a "0" then the data will be right justified
-u	A switch that causes all date operations to be performed in universal standard time (UTC)

See also: crontab, time

dc

```
dc file
```

This command is a simple line-oriented desk calculator. It can perform multiple math operations using the common reverse Polish notation (RPN) found in many calculators. For example,

```
$   dc
    1
    2
    +
    p
    3
```

df

```
df [-t] [-f] [-b] [-l|-L] file_systems
...
```

This command provides information on your filesystems. For instance, keying df by itself displays use statistics for all filesystems currently mounted.

Categories are as follows:

○   **Filesystem**: the name of the filesystems.

○   **Device:** the device name or host the filesystem resides on.

○   **avail:** the number of 512-byte blocks available on the device.

○   **inodes**: the number of i-nodes available on the device.

When a filesystem is mounted, its root directory becomes the subdirectory on which the system is mounted. The filesystem's tree then becomes subdirectories of the mount point.

For instance, assume that you mount an external disk containing two directories, /letters and /status.maint, and you mount the disk on your /exports subdirectory. The pathnames to the two external subdirectories would then be /exports/letters and /exports/status.maint.

Switches and Options:

-t   Reports on the total allocated blocks as well.

-f   Only reports the free block count (not the i-nodes).

-b   Reports total number of blocks allocated as
            well as the total number of blocks free for
            swapping to the filesystem.

-l   In an HP cluster environment, reports file-
            systems mounted on the local c-node.

-L   In an HP cluster environment, reports the
            filesystems that may be unmounted from the
            local c-node.

Remarks and Cautions:

In an NFS environment, the number of i-nodes reported for
a remote filesystem may be -1. This will happen if the remote
filesystem has not exported root permissions to your system.

☞ *CAUTION: All space is described in 512-byte blocks.
Some of the best administrators I know have misread
them and filled their disk up unexpectedly.*

See also: du, bdf

diff

```
diff [-C n] [-S name] [-lrs]
[-bcefhintw] dir1 dir2

diff [-C n] [-S name] [-bcefhintw] file1
file2

diff [-D string] [-biw] file1 file2
```

This command compares files and reports on their differences. If diff is used to compare directories, then the filenames in the two directories are sorted, and files with the same names between the two directories are compared.

Switches and Options:

-l	Long output format.
-r	Applies diff recursively to any subdirectories found with the same name.
-s	Reports files that are identical.
-S name	Starts a sorted directory compare with the filename provided.
-e	Produces an ed script suitable for converting file1 into file2.
-f	Produces a diff script (like that produced by the -e) that is easier to read.
-n	Produces a script, similar to the one produced by -e, that is the same form produced by rcsdiff.
-c	Produces an output form that is slightly different from the standard diff format and that contains three lines of context.
-C n	Produces a list that's the same format as produced by the -c, except with n lines of context.

-h   Does a fast, simple listing of the differences.
                 This only works when the changes between
                 the files are simple and well delineated.

-D *string*   Produces a merged version of the two files
                 on the standard output, with C preprocessor
                 directives defined such that when string is
                 defined, the compile results in file2 being
                 used. Without string defined, file1 will be
                 used.

-b   Ignores trailing blanks.

-w   Ignores all white space.

-i   Ignores uppercase/lowercase differences.

-t   Expands tabs in the output listing.

Other Uses and Suggestions:

When comparing large text files, it might be handy to redirect
the output of the diff to another file. For instance,

    $ diff hpux.intro hpux.notes diff.report

dirname

dirname *string*

dirname removes the leaf name from a supplied pathname and returns the directory portion of the pathname. If a directory pathname isn't provided with the pathname, a "." will be returned to indicate the local working directory.

    $ basename /usr/tmp/junk.wk1
         /usr/tmp

See also: basename

dmesg

```
dmesg [-]
```

This command collects system diagnostic messages for use in troubleshooting. For instance,

```
$    dmesg ↵
```

displays system diagnostic messages on the screen.

Switches and Options:

Collects system diagnostic messages since the last time it was run and displays them on standard output.

Remarks and Cautions:

Only root can run dmesg. It's common to have a root cron job scheduled to write dmesg output to /usr/adm/messages as follows:

```
0,10,20,30,40,50 * * * * /etc/dmesg - >>
/usr/adm/messages
```

domainname

        domainname *name*

This command displays or sets the current network information service (NIS) name. For instance,

    $ domainname↵

would display the name of the current NIS domain.

Remarks and Cautions:

Only a superuser can set a domain name. Usually, it is set
during an NIS installation.

Other Uses and Suggestions:

domainname is useful in scripts written in multi-domain
environments.

dos2ux

```
dos2ux file ...
```

This command converts files from MS-DOS to UNIX format. It is particularly useful for preparing text files for use on your workstation after they were edited on a computer running DOS.

dos2ux reads each filename provided and writes them to standard output as they are converted. If no filenames are provided, then the input file will be taken from standard in and the result will be written to standard output. For instance,

```
$    dos2ux <test.txt>text.TXT.
```

converts the file test.txt in DOS format to a UNIX file with the name test.TXT.

See also: ux2dos

doscp

```
doscp [-fvu] file1 file2
```

This command copies a file to or from a DOS format floppy. Filenames for the DOS media must be legal DOS names. Also, the pathname for the DOS file is a colon-separated combination of the floppy device file and the DOS filesystem pathname for the file (using UNIX forward slashes to separate the parts of the pathname). For example,

```
$   doscp mywork.wk1
    /dev/rfloppy/c201d1s0:mywork.wk1↵
```

Switches and Options:

-f	Unconditionally writes over anything at the destination with the same name.
-v	Verbose mode.
-u	Disables filename conversion. (Doesn't convert pathnames to uppercase.)

See also: ux2dos, dos2ux, dosls, dosdf

dosdf

dosdf *device:*

This command reports the number of free disk clusters on a DOS-formatted disk in the floppy drive. This is the DOS analog to the UNIX df or bdf commands.

See also: ux2dos, dos2ux, dosls, doscp, dosmkdir, df, bdf

dosls

dosls [-aAudl] *device:file*

This command displays a listing of the files in a DOS filesystem. For instance,

$ dosls /dev/rfloppy/c201d1s0:/↵

Switches and Options:

-a	Lists all directories including the hidden files.
-A	Same as -a except the current and parent directory listings aren't shown.
-u	Doesn't convert DOS filenames to upper-case.
-d	If a listed file is a directory, only displays its name and not its contents.
-l	Displays the output in long format.

See also: ux2dos, dos2ux, doscp, dosdf, dosmkdir

dosmkdir

dosmkdir *device:directory*

This command makes a directory on a DOS format floppy.

$ dosmkdir /dev/rfloppy/c201d1s0:/mydir↵

Switches and Options:

- u   Disables DOS filename conversion to upper-
                case.

See also: ux2dos, dos2ux, dosls, doscp,
          dosdf, mkdir

dosrm

dosrm [-friu] *device:file* ...

This command removes a file from a DOS format floppy disk.

Switches and Options:

-f   Forces the deletion.

-r   Causes dosrm to recursively delete the entire directory tree.

-i   Causes dosrm to interactively ask about each file it is to delete.

-u   Doesn't perform the conversion of DOS filenames to uppercase.

See also: doscp, dosdf, dosrmdir, mkdir

dosrmdir

dosrmdir *device:dirname* ...

This command removes an empty directory from a DOS filesystem.

Switches and Options:

-u   Doesn't perform the conversion of DOS filenames to uppercase.

See also: doscp, dosdf, dosrm

du

du [-a|-s] [-brx] [-t *type*] *file* ...

This command reports the number of 512-byte disk blocks used by a filesystem. For instance,

    $ du -s /users/jrice↵

would report on disk usage only for files in the directory /usrs/jrice.

Switches and Options:

-a	Reports disk utilization for each file in the hierarchies in addition to the normal output.
-b	For each file in a directory for which swap has been enabled, reports the number of blocks that swap is currently using.
-r	Prints messages about directories that can't be read.
-s	Prints only the utilization summary.
-x	Limits the report to the disk usage on the same device as the base directory specification. (Doesn't report information for directories that may be mounted under the base directory.)
-t *type*	Restricts usage reporting to files that are members of filesystems that are of the *type* indicated.

See also: bdf, df

echo

```
echo args
```

This command writes, for instance, the following line in a
.profile script:

```
$    echo Good Morning, Mary Ellen!↵
```

This would cheerfully greet Mary Ellen each morning when
she logs into the system.

Switches and Options:

echo also understands a number of special formatting commands that can be used to format its output. (Be careful not
to run into conflicts with the shell's use of the backslash
character.)

\b	Backspace.
\c	Print line without appending a new-line.
\f	Form-feed.
\n	New-line.
\r	Carriage return.
\t	Tab.
\v	Vertical tab.
\\	Backslash.
\n	The 8-bit character whose ASCII code is the octal number n (the first digit must be zero).

env

```
env [-] [-i] [name=value] [command
[arguments]]
```

This command displays and/or modifies variables in the environment for the execution of the given command. When env is used without a command or any arguments, it will display the current environment variables. For instance,

```
$    env↵
```

displays a list of all global environment variables and their values.

```
$    env VERSION=1 run.script
```

executes the script run.script with the environment variable VERSION set equal to 1.

Switches and Options:

name=value   Sets the named environment variable to value.

-i   Ignores the current environment and executes the command with only the environment that is setup with the env command.

-    An obsolete version of the -i switch.

command   Used with the name=value argument; sets the new value, then executes the command.

Remarks and Cautions:

This command is useful for temporarily changing an environment variable before executing a command that will use the new value.

expand

```
expand [-tabstop] [-tab1,tab2,...,tabn]
filename ...
```

This command expands tab characters to spaces such that each tabbed column begins in specified columns. When a single *tabstop* is used, tabs are set at *tabstop* increments instead of the default 8. For instance,

```
$   expand -5,18,35 file.txt↵
```

would place tabbed positions in columns 5, 18, and 35 in file.txt.

Switches and Options:

-tabstop   Places tabstops at the defined increments; the default is 8.

-tab1,tab2,...,tabn
                    Numeric values for number of spaces to replace each tab character.

Remarks and Cautions:

expand follows these rules:

○   If no *tab#* is specified, expand defaults to column tabulation at 8 character boundaries.

○   If multiple *tab#* are specified, expand places a tab column at each *tabpos*, just as it would if you set multiple tabs in your word processor ruler line.

See also: unexpand

factor

factor *number*

This command evaluates the factors of the given number. If no number is given as an argument, then factor waits for numbers to be entered on the standard input. This isn't the most useful program in the world, but it is something of a UNIX tradition.

See also: primes

file

file [-m *mfile*] [-c] [-f *ffile*] *filename*

This command determines a file type, whether a text, an executable, or a program. For instance,

```
$    file escher.ps⏎
     escher.ps: postscript file
```

Switches and Options:

-m   Instructs file to use *mfile* as an alternative to the magic file located in /etc/magic.

-c   Instructs file to check the magic file for format errors.

-f *ffile* Tells file to check all files listed in the specified file containing a list of files to be checked.

Remarks and Cautions:

Occasionally, file misinterprets a command file as a C language program. It has been known to misinterpret PostScript files as YACC files.

> ✔ *TIP:* If you only want to check a few files, rather than creating a filelist or repeating the *file* command, just name the files as arguments to *file*. For example,

```
$    file /dev /etc/hosts $HOME/escher.ps
     /dev: directory
     /etc/hosts: ascii text
     /users/jrice/escher.ps: postscript file
```

See also: find, ls

find

find *path-name-list expression*

This command searches the pathname for files (including subdirectories) that match the expression. For instance,

$ find / -user jrice -perm 644 -print↵

searches all filesystems, beginning with the root directory, for files that belong to jrice, carry read permission for everyone, write permission for only jrice, and execute permission for no one; then prints all of the matching pathnames to standard output.

Switches and Options:

-depth	Searches subdirectories of *start_path-6name* before searching *start_path-name*.
-follow	Causes find to follow symbolic links.
-hidden	Causes find to search hidden directories.
-fsonly *type*	Causes find to stop descent into directories that are not of the given filesystem type.
-xdev	A switch that causes find not to descend into directories that are mounted below the base search path.
-mountstop	Same as -xdev. Provided for backward compatibility with older versions of find.
-name *file*	True if file matches the last component of the current pathname.
-path *file*	Like -name except that the full pathname is used in the match rather than the basename.
-perm *mode*	True if the mode of the pathname being examined matches the mode provided. (See chmod for a more detailed description of possible values for mode.)

-fstype *type*	True if the filesystem that the file belongs to is of the given type.
-type c	True if the file is of the given type. Type can be one of the following: d, directory; b, block special file; c, character special device; p, FIFO (named pipe); l, symbolic link; s, socket; n, network special file; M, mount point; H, hidden directory.
-links *n*	True if file has *n* number of references in the filesystem directories (otherwise referred to as "hard links").
-user *uname*	True if the file is owned by the user, *uname*.
-group *gname*	True if the file is owned by the group, *gname*.
-devcid *cname*	True if the file is a block or character device special file that belongs to the c-node, *cname*.
-nouser	True if the file is owned by a user who's not listed in the passwd database file.
-nogroup	True if the file is owned by a group that's not listed in the group database file.
-nodevcid	True if the device file is owned by a c-node not listed in the /etc/clusterconf file.
-size *n*[c]	True if the file is *n* blocks long. If *n* is followed by a c, then the size is in characters.
-atime *n*	Returns true if file has been accessed in past *n* days.
-ctime *n*	Returns true if file has been changed in past *n* days.
-newer *filename*	Returns true if file has modification time later than *filename*.

-newer[acm[acm]] *filename*

Returns True if the indicated time value for the file is later than filename. The time attribute of the file that will be used is determined by the acm fields on the switch. The a represents the last access time of the file, the c represents the last time the i-node was modified, and the m represents the last time the file was modified. The first acm specifies the time of the current file and the second acm specifies the time on the file-name.

-inum *n*   Returns true if file has i-node number n.

-linkedto *path*   True if the file is the same physical file as the file specified by path. This switch is used to detect files that are hardlinked to-gether.

-print   Causes find to print the search result to standard output.

$-3-exec command   Executes command on matching files. The command can include the name of the file by using the double bracket [{}] to mark where the pathname is to be included. Also, the command must always be terminated with a semi-colon. Since the semi-colon is a shell special character, you will probably have to escape it with a backslash (\); for example:

    #   find / -user jrice -exec chown markt {}
         \;↵

-ok *command*   Interactive version of -exec; waits for "y" from user before executing command.

-cpio *device*   Writes the current file on *device* in cpio format.

-ncpio *device*   Same as cpio but adds the -c option to cpio.

-prune   Stops find from descending into the tree.

-only   This is a positive-logic version of -prune.

-acl *acl_pattern* True if the file matches the *acl_pattern* provided.

Remarks and Cautions:

It's worth a little time to become familiar with this command; it is one of the most flexible and powerful in the suite. A very specific search can be set up by careful application of the various arguments.

See also: chgrp, chmod, cpio, file, grep, ls, ln

finger

```
finger [-bfilmpqRsw] username
```

This command delivers more detail than who. For instance,

```
$  finger⏎
```

displays information about all users logged into the machine.

Switches and Options:

-b	Causes finger not to display the user's home directory or shell.
-f	Causes finger not to display the header of the report.
-i	Reports only the login name, terminal, login time, and idle time.
-l	Displays a long format: login name, real name, home directory, shell, login time and location, when mail was last read, and contents of /.plan and /.projects.
-m	Matches only username.
-p	Doesn't display the contents of a users $HOME/.plan file.
-q	Causes finger to generate a quick report listing only the login name, terminal, and login times.
-R	Prints the user's hostname.
-s	Displays a short form: login name, real name, terminal name, idle time, and when and where logged in.
-w	Causes finger not to display the full name in a short form output.

See also: w, who, whoami

fold

```
fold [-s] [-w width] file ...
```

This command wraps lines in a wide file into output that's limited to a specified number of characters, for example, a printer.

Switches and Options:

-s   Breaks the line on the last white space before the output width is reached.

-w width   Defines the maximum width of the output.

from

```
from [-s sender] username
```

This command displays mail headers from your or another user's mailbox. For instance,

```
$    from↵
```

lists headers for your mailbox.

Switches and Options:

$-3-s *sender*   Lists headers for mail in your mailbox sent to you by the specified sender.

username   Lists headers for mail in a mailbox for the specified *username*. Of course, you must have permission to read the user's mailbox that you specify.

See also: mail, mailx

ftp

`ftp [-ginv]` *hostname*

This command is a file transfer protocol for transferring files to and from a remote host. For instance,

`$   ftp -i farmton↵`

would initiate a connection to host name `farmton`, without interactive prompting during the actual file transfers.

`ftp` is an interactive file transfer facility that provides the user with a command line prompt that accepts commands for connecting to remote hosts, obtaining lists of files and directories on remote systems, sending files to the remote system, or pulling files from the remote system.

More detailed help on the interactive commands available within the `ftp` facility can be obtained by typing `help` at any `ftp` prompt.

Switches and Options:

`-g`	Disables the expansion of wildcard in filenames; filenames will be taken literally.
`-i`	Turns off interactive prompting during transfer of multiple files.
`-n`	Disables automatic login; otherwise would use `.netrc` file.
`-v`	Shows all responses from the remote host (this is the default switch).

See also: `rcp`, `telnet`

grep

```
grep [-E | -F] [-cilnqsvx] [pattern]
file ...

grep [-E | -F] [-cilnqsvx] -e pattern
[-e pattern ...] file ...

grep [-E | -F] [-cilnqsvx] [-f
pattern_file] file ...
```

This command searches specified files for strings or expressions. For instance,

```
$    grep -i Jim PhoneList.txt⏎
```

Switches and Options:

-E	Uses extended regular expressions.
-F	Uses fixed string specifications.
-b	Precedes each line with a matching pattern with the block number it was located in.
-c	Displays total number of matching lines rather than the lines themselves.
-e *expression*	Uses expression as the pattern to search for. Multiple -e switches may be used to search for multiple expressions. The -e switch can also be used to search for patterns that begin with a -.
-f *pattern_file*	All regular expressions that will be searched for are taken from the *pattern_file*.
-i	Ignores case during search.
-l	Lists filenames only of files with matching lines.
-n	Precedes each matching line with its line number.

-q	Executes quietly, with nothing sent to standard output. Exits with a zero status once the first match has been found.
-s	Suppresses warning messages about files that aren't found.
-v	Displays lines that don't match rather than those that do.
-x	Exacts matches of the entire line are required.

Remarks and Cautions:

grep searches for strings, that is, a search for "and" will find "and," "band," and "andover." Of course, it won't find "Andover" unless you use -i to ignore case. To grep the word "and," place it and its surrounding spaces inside quotes; e.g.,

        $ grep ' and ' *filename*

To grep a word at the beginning of a line, as the word "Help" in "Help me make it through the night," use a caret, e.g.,

        $ grep ^Help *filename*

To grep a string at the end of a line, use a $, e.g.,

        $ grep night$ *filename*

To grep a word beginning with either upper- or lowercase,

        $ grep [Vv]ineyard] *filename*

To grep a string beginning with any lowercase letter,

        $ grep [a-z]*rest_of_string*

To grep a string beginning with any uppercase letter,

        $ grep [A-Z]*rest_of_string*

To grep any character in a string,

        $

```
grep str.ng filename which would return
"string" and "strong."
```

To grep characters that grep would otherwise recognize as a special character, precede the character with a \.

See also: file, find

groups

groups [-p] [-g] [-1] *username*

This command displays a user's group memberships as defined in the /etc/passwd, /etc/group, and /etc/logingroup files. For instance,

$ groups⏎

would display all the groups to which you belong. Add username to the command to see group memberships for that user.

Switches and Options:

-p   Limits the list of groups to those listed in the /etc/passwd file.

-g   Limits the list of groups to those listed in the /etc/group file.

-1   Limits the list of groups to those listed in the /etc/logingroup file.

See also: newgrp

head

head [-c | -l] [-n *count*] *file* ...

This command displays the first few lines of a file. For instance,

$ head LongList.txt

would display the first 10 lines of the file called Long-List.txt.

Switches and Options:

-c   Measures the output quantity in bytes rather than lines.

-l   Measures the output quantity in lines; this is the default.

-n *count*   Causes head to display the first count lines (or bytes if used with -c) of the specified file.

Remarks and Cautions:

This command accepts wildcards. For instance,

$ head -5 .*

would display the first 5 lines of all system files in the current working directory. Each filename is shown as follows: ==> filename <== .

See also: cat, more, tail

hostname

```
hostname name
```

This command displays or sets the current host's name.

Switches and Options:

name

Sets hostname to name; usually done by the start-up script /etc/rc, though it can be set by a superuser.

hp-pa

```
hp-pa
```

This command returns a true or false, depending on the architecture of the machine. For instance,

```
$    if [hp-pa]; then echo "I'm a PA RISC
     computer" ; fi
```

```
I'm a PA RISC computer
```

This if statement, executed on a PA-RISC computer series 700 or series 800, illustrates how the hp-pa command may be used to conditionally execute commands for the PA-RISC architecture.

Switches and Options:

The hp-pa command has no switches or options.

Computers based on the System V interface definition all host architecture-specific commands such as hp-pa. Other examples of this type of command are hp9000s200, hp9000s300, hp9000s400, hp9000s500, hp9000s700, hp9000s800, hp-mc680x0, pdp11, u3b, and vax.

id

```
id [-g | -u] [-nr] user
```

This command displays your or someone else's userid,
groupid, and ids and names of other groups to which you
belong.

Switches and Options:

-g	Outputs the groupid only.
-u	Outputs the userid only.
-n	Outputs the name instead of the numeric id of the groupid or userid.
-r	Outputs the real id rather than the effective id of the user.
user	Outputs information about the specified user rather than yourself.

See also: chgrp

kill

```
kill [-1]

kill [-signo | - signame] pid
```

This command kills specified processes.

Switches and Options:

-1   Displays a list of signal numbers and their associated signal names that are available on the system.

-signo   Sends the type of signal to the process specified by the number indicated by signo.

-signame   Sends the type of signal to the process specified by the name indicated by signame.

Remarks and Cautions:

Determine the process identification number (pid) from the second field in a ps command display line. Determine the signal number by running kill -1 and counting the position of the desired signal name. For instance,

```
$   kill -1
```

```
 1) HUP     16) USR1
 2) INT     17) USR2
 3) QUIT    18) CHLD
 4) ILL     19) PWR
 5) TRAP    20) VTALRM
 6) IOT     21) PROF
 7) EMT     22) POLL
 8) FPE     23) WINCH
 9) KILL    24) STOP
10) BUS     25) TSTP
11) SEGV    26) CONT
12) SYS     27) TTIN
13) PIPE    28) TTOU
14) ALRM    29) URG
15) TERM    30) LOST
```

To ensure the death of process 389, enter

```
$   kill -9 389
```

which kills the process. (Some processes don't die easily. However, using this strong a signal should be done with caution!)

See also: ps, grep

last

```
last [-c] [-R] [-count] name ... [tty
...]
```

This command reports information on the previous work sessions for the specified user or system interface. For instance,

```
$   last -25↵
```

displays the last 25 sessions for your computer, most recent session first.

Switches and Options:

-c	Directs last to display information about all computers in the HP-UX cluster.
-R	Directs last to display the hostname of the system that was the source of a connection originated through the network.
-count	Directs last to display only the number of connections specified by count.
user	Restricts last to list information about this user.

✓ *TIP: You may specify multiple users by separating their usernames with a space.*

tty	Like user, this option specifies a tty or tty type to display.

leave

`leave [hhmm]`

This is an appointment reminder.

Switches and Options:

`hhmm`   Hours and minutes, 12-hour format.

Remarks and Cautions:

Entering `leave` by itself results in the query: What time do you have to leave? You respond with an absolute hour-minute time. `leave` assumes the time to be within the upcoming 12 hours (so you can't leave a reminder this morning for tomorrow morning). It warns you with the following messages:

○   (Beep!) Just one more minute!

○   (Beep!) Time to leave!

○   (Beep!) You're going to be late!

○   (Beep!) That was the last time I'll tell you. Bye.

`leave` warns you of your impending tardiness every minute until 10 minutes after the appointment time.

See also: `cal, calendar`

ln

```
ln [-f] [-i] [-s] file1 new_file

ln [-f] [-i] [-s] file1 [file2 ...]
dest_directory

ln [-f] [-i] [-s] dir1 [dir2 ...]
dest_directory
```

This command creates a new reference, called a link, to an existing file or directory.

There are two basic types of links, soft-links and hard-links. A soft-link may reference objects on filesystems other than the one that contains the link, it may point to directories, and it may point toward an object that may not even exist.

A hard-link may only reference objects on the same filesystem that the link resides on, it may only reference files and not directories (unless you are the superuser, and even then you probably shouldn't do it), and it can only exist if the file that the link references actually exists.

A link allows files or directories with different names to point to the same data. For instance, if one user wants to name a file address.clients and another prefers to call the same file simply clients, the two files could be linked so that each user would call a different filename, yet be working with the same information.

For example, you could create a link in your home directory that points to a file in some other directory or filesystem, thus saving yourself some keying when you want to call the file.

Similarly, you could create a link in your home directory that points to another directory. When you list your directory using the ls command, you would actually be looking at the link_source directory. For example,

```
$   ln /users/reports/jan/summary.sales
    $HOME/sales.⏎
```

would create a link named sales in your home directory that would point to the file /users/reports/jan/summary.sales. Any edits you perform on the sales file would be reflected in /users/reports/jan/summary.sales, since you are actually editing that file.

Switches and Options:

-f	Performs the ln command without prompting for permission.
-i	Interactively prompts the user if the resulting link object would overwrite an existing file.
-s	Creates a symbolic link.

Remarks and Cautions:

✔ **TIP:** Use *ln* instead of *cp* when edits made to a file by multiple users must be reflected in everyone's copy of that file.

⮕ **NOTE:** *cp allows copies of a file to be made so that multiple users start with the same data, but all copies are not updated when edits are made. When files are linked, all members of the link structure are updated when any member is changed.*

⮕ **NOTE:** *Links may be removed with the rm command.*

What is actually removed from the disk depends on the type of link that's being deleted. If rm is used on a soft-link, then the link is the only thing removed. The file itself is only removed when it is deleted through the use of its original filename. If the file is removed before the soft-link is removed, the soft-link will be left pointing to nothing at all.

When rm is used on a hard-link, only the reference to the file is removed unless it represents the very last reference to the file. If the hard-link is the last reference, then the file itself, along with the hard-link, will be removed from the disk. This is true even if the original filename is deleted from the filesystem. As long as a hard-link is left to reference the file, the file will be left on the disk.

See also: cp, rm

login

```
login [username env_var ...]
```

This command initiates the sequence by which a user is permitted to use a machine. A username can be provided when the command is invoked, or `login` will request it. If additional environment variables are desired in the user's login environment, they may be assigned explicitly on the `login` command line. If `login` is invoked as a command, then it must be initiated as a top-level process, as follows:

```
$    exec login jrice↵
```

will initiate `login` for a user recognized by the system as jrice.

> ✏ **NOTE:** If keyed without a username, `login` will prompt for a username.

Switches and Options:

-p   Preserves any existing environment variables; otherwise, any previous environment table is overwritten.

Remarks and Cautions:

`login` provides user-level security by limiting access to only those users who have been granted access by the system administrator. After you key in your username, `login` will prompt for your password. If the username and password you enter are valid and correct, the system will log into your home directory and execute the commands in your `$HOME/.profile` file. See the login chapter for more information on that process.

See also: `passwd, su`

---

ls

`ls [-abcdfgilmnopqrstuxACFHLR1]` *names*

This command displays the names and attributes of files and directories contained in the directory that you specify. If you don't specify specific filenames or directories to examine, `ls` will list the contents and attributes of the files in your current working directory. It also has to have more switches than any other single command in UNIX.

Switches and Options:

- `-a`   Lists all entries in the directory including the hidden files. A hidden file is one that is not normally displayed in a directory listing because it starts with a period (such as your `.profile`).

- `-b`   Displays nonprintable characters as octal numbers.

- `-c`   Uses last modification time of the object for sorting.

- `-d`   If the name is a directory, `-d` only lists it and not its contents.

- `-f`   Forces all entries to be evaluated as a directory.

- `-g`   **Prints the file's group ownership.**

- `-i`   Prints the i-node number associated with the file.

- `-l`   Lists the output in long format.

- `-m`   Streams output format.

- `-n`   Prints the owners' uid and gid numbers rather than owners' names.

- `-o`   Same as `-l` except only the owner and not the group is printed.

- `-p`   Prints a slash after names that are really directories.

-q	Displays nonprintable characters in filenames as a question mark.
-r	Reverses the order of the sort rather than the default alphabetical order.
-s	Gives the size of the file in 512-byte blocks.
-t	Sorts the list by the time modified.
-u	Sorts the list by the last access time.
-x	Sorts multicolumn output across the page rather than down.
-A	Same as -a except "." and ".." aren't displayed.
-C	Sorts multicolumn output down the page rather than across.
-F	Puts a slash (/) after the directory names, an asterisk (*) after the executables, an at sign (@) after the symbolic links to files, and a pipe (I) after FIFOs.
-H	Puts a plus after each file that is a context-dependant file (cdf).
-L	If the object is a link to a directory, displays the directory rather than the link.
-R	Lists the contents of the directory specified and all subdirectories found underneath it.
-1	Lists all the output in a single column. *NOTE: This command comes in a number of forms for easier typing.*
l	Same as ls -m.
ll	Same as ls -l.
lsf	Same as ls -F.
lsr	Same as ls -R.
lsx	Same as ls -x.

mail

```
mail [+] [-epqr] [-f file]

mail [-dt] person ...
```

This command activates electronic mail. This particular version of e-mail uses a text-based interface. For instance,

```
$  mail + ↵
```

prints the oldest mail in your mailbox and then prompts you for a command. You can see a summary of the available commands by typing a question mark.

To view a particular message, enter its number. To send mail, type the command mail, followed by the address in the form *user@host*.

Switches and Options:

+	Displays the messages from oldest to newest.
-e	Suppresses printing of mail and returns a status indicating whether there is new mail waiting.
-p	Prints all mail without waiting for command entry.
-q	Terminates mail if an interrupt signal is caught.
-r	Same as the +.
-f *mailfile*	Causes mail to view the file instead of the default /usr/mail.
-t	Causes a copy of the mail message to be sent to the user who is sending the mail.

- d   Causes mail to be delivered directly rather
              than passed to the sendmail routing agent.
              (Normally this feature is only used by send-
              mail itself and not by the user.)

See also: mailx

mailx

```
mailx [-d] [-e] [-f filename] [-F]
[-h number] [-H] [-i] [-n] [-N] [-r
address] [-s subject] [-u user] [-U]
destination_address
```

This command provides a standard System V command line mail interface to read and send electronic mail. A number of command line options exist to control its behavior. Also, there is a rich command set that can be used to interactively control mailx's operation. A summary of the interactive commands can be listed once mailx has been invoked by typing the question mark.

Switches and Options:

-d	Turns on debugging output (ridiculously verbose).
-e	Tests for the presence of mail. Prints nothing, then exits.
-f filename	Reads mail from the given filename rather than the default mailbox in /usr/mail.
-F	Records the message in a file that has a name that's the same as the first recipient of the message.
-h number	Explicitly declares the number of network hops made by the mail.
-H	Only prints a list of the mail headers.
-i	Ignores interrupts received from the shell.
-n	Doesn't use the default system mailx.rc file. The mail.rc file defined the default options and configuration values for the mailx tool.
-N	Doesn't print out the initial summary of messages.

-r *address* Passes the address given directly to send-mail.

-s *subject* Defines the content of the "Subject:" header for the mail. If the subject is to contain white space, it must be contained in quotes.

-u *user* Reads another user's mailbox. This isn't very useful since the default on most systems is to keep a user's mailbox protected.

-U Converts old style UUCP style addresses (*hostname!user*) to Internet style addresses (*user@hostname*).

See also: mail

man

```
man [-] [section[subsection]] entry_name

man -f file ...

man -k keyword ...
```

This command displays information from the reference manuals. man can display an individual manual entry, or with the -k *option*, it can display a list of manual pages that match the supplied keyword. For instance,

```
$   man -k telnet
    telnet(1)-user interface to the TELNET
    protocol
    telnetd(1m) - TELNET protocol server
```

The first column contains the title of the command with the section number in parentheses. The second column contains a brief description of the entry.

> **NOTE:** *If you are going to use the* -k *option, it's important that your system administrator has run the catman facility on your workstation's manual pages. Catman must be run in order to build the cross-reference file used by* man -k.

Switches and Options:

-k   Performs a keyword search and displays man pages that match.

section[subsection]Defines the section that should be searched for the man page.

Remarks and Cautions:

If there are multiple manual entries with the same title, you may need to specify the section to search. For a complete listing of the various sections and their definitions, read the man manual page—try man man.

mesg

```
mesg [y | n]
```

This commands controls whether messages can be displayed
to your terminal. If no argument is used to mesg, then the
current value will be displayed. For instance,

```
$    mesg n
```

deactivates the message display.

mkdir

```
mkdir [-p] [-m mode] dirname...
```

This command creates a new directory.

```
$   mkdir misc-stuff
```

Switches and Options:

-m   Specifies the mode to be assigned to the newly created directory.

-p   Creates all directories specified in the path-name that don't exist.

Remarks and Cautions:

Before you can create a directory, you must have write permission (and the right permissions) in the parent directory.

mktemp

[-c] [-d *directory_name*] [-p *prefix*]

This command generates a name for a temporary file. The mktemp command doesn't actually create a file, it only generates a unique filename that can be used without having to worry about overwriting someone else's files. This is a very handy thing to have when working with shell scripts.

```
$    tempname=`mktemp`
$    dosomething $tempname
```

Switches and Options:

-c
Generates a zero length file using the names generated.

-d *directory_name*
Uses *directory_name* to generate the pathname. The default is /tmp.

-p *prefix*
Uses prefix as the leading part of the temporary filename leaf.

more

```
more [-n] [-cdflsu] [ +lineno ]
[+/ pattern] filename ...
```

This command displays the contents of a file one screenful at a time.

Switches and Options:

-n	Uses a window size of n lines.
-c	Writes each page from the beginning of the screen.
-d	Prompts the user for an action at the bottom of each screen.
-f	Doesn't automatically fold long lines.
-l	Ignores the form-feed character.
-u	Ignores underlining.
-s	Replaces multiple blank lines with a single blank line.
+lineno	Starts displaying file at line number *line-number*.
+/pattern	Starts displaying file two lines prior to the first match of *pattern*.

Remarks and Cautions:

The following keys are used to page through the file:

ENTER	Moves display down one line.
SPACE	Displays the next screenful of text.
control-D	Displays the next 1/2 screenful of text.
q or Q	Exits more.
h	Describes all commands that more accepts.

mount

mount *device directory*

This command is used to make an external filesystem available on a given directory. In effect, it grafts the contents of that directory to the named directory. For instance,

    $ mount /dev/dsk/c201d3s0 /exports/3s0

mounts a disk drive from device /dev/dsk/c201d3s0 and appends it to the /exports/3s0 directory. This command can also be used to mount a CD-ROM, floppy disk, or magneto-optical drive. Entering the command without arguments displays a list of currently mounted filesystems.

☞ *NOTE: You must be logged in as the superuser to use the* mount *command.*

See also: umount

mv

```
mv [-f] [-i] filename1 [filename2 ...]
target
```

This command moves a file from filename1 to target, or moves a list of files to a directory target. For example,

```
$   mv README README.OLD
```

moves the file README from the current directory to the file named README.OLD, also in the current directory. Moving all files that end in payroll is just as easy:

```
$   mv *payroll MAY-data
```

moves all files that end in the string payroll to the directory MAY-data.

Switches and Options:

-i   Prompts for action if the move will overwrite a file.

-f   Forces the move. Overwrites any existing files. Overrides the -i option.

Remarks and Cautions:

To rename a file, just move it to the new name in the same directory.

newgrp

`newgrp [-]` *groupname*

This command changes the current user's group membership. (The current user is whoever is logged into the system.) Before a user can change a group, the user must be a member of that group in the `/etc/group` database. If the user is not a member of the group and the group has a password in the `/etc/group` file, then the user will be prompted for this password before being changed to that group.

If the - is used in the `newgrp` command, then the user's `.profile` (or `.cshrc`) file will be executed with the start of the new shell. For instance,

`$    newgrp ipg`

changes the logged-in user to the group "ipg." Entering `newgrp` without an argument reverts the user to his or her original group.

Remarks and Cautions:

Groups specified must previously have been created by the system administrator.

See also: `chgrp, whoami, groups, id`

page

```
page [-n] [-cdflsu] [+linenumber]
[+/pattern] name ...
```

This command displays a text file on the display, one screenful at a time. For instance,

```
$   page -cdr /testfile.text
```

displays the contents of testfile.text, clearing the screen after each new screenful, prompting the user to press a key to continue, and forcing display of all ASCII characters.

> 📝 **NOTE:** *This command is nearly identical to* more. *The only difference is that* page *clears the screen between every screenful of text.*

Switches and Options:

-n	Uses a window size of n lines.
-c	Writes each page from the beginning of the screen.
-d	Prompts the user for an action at the bottom of each screen.
-f	Doesn't automatically fold long lines.
-l	Ignores the form feed character.
-u	Ignores underlining.
-s	Replaces multiple blank lines with a single blank line.
+lineno	Starts displaying file at line number *linenumber.*
+/pattern	Starts displaying file two lines prior to the first match of *pattern.*

Remarks and Cautions:

The following keys are used to page through the file:

ENTER   Moves display down one line.

SPACE   Moves display down 1 screenful.

control-D   Moves display 1/2 page down.

q or Q   Exits page.

h   Describes all commands that page accepts.

See also: more

passwd

passwd [-f *file*] *name*

This command is used to change a user's password. If the specified user has no password, the command can be used to assign a new one. For instance,

$ passwd

invokes an interactive procedure, where the machine requests the new password and asks for it to be entered again to confirm.

Switches and Options:

-f   Chooses an alternate file for password to operate on. The default is /etc/password.

Remarks and Cautions:

Only superusers can change the passwords of users other than their own.

Other Uses and Suggestions:

A superuser does not need to know a user's old password in order to change it. Thus, a superuser can use this command to assign a new password to a user who has forgotten his or her old one.

See also: su, whoami, yppasswd

paste

```
paste file1 file2

-d list file1 file2

-s [-d list] file1 file2
```

This command appends corresponding lines of each file together to form a single line and prints out the result.

Switches and Options:

-d *list*	Causes the list to be used as the separator between the lines of the files that paste is operating on. The default is a tab. If the list is more than one character long, the first character will be used as the first delimeter, the second character as the second delimiter, etc.
list	The characters that are used to separate the lines that have been pasted together.
-s	Merges adjacent lines in the given files together.

See also: cut

pg

```
pg [-number] [-p string] [-cefns]
[+1 linenumber] [+/pattern/] file ...
```

This command is used to display a text file on a display, one page at a time. It differs from other screen pagers in that it allows a user to display backward as well as forward into a file.

Switches and Options:

-number	Uses number as the number of lines on the display.
,,-p string	Uses string as the prompt.
-c	Clears the display between each page of the text file.
-e	When multiple files are given, tells pg not to stop between files.
-f	Tells pg not to split lines that are wider than the display.
-n	Ends the command when the end of command letter is detected.
-s	Tells pg not to use inverse video to display commands.
+1 linenumber	Tells pg to start the display at the specific linenumber of the file.
+/pattern/	Starts listing at the first occurrence of pattern.

A summary of commands that can be used by pg interactively can be found by typing an h at the prompt.

See also: page, more

primes

```
primes [start[stop]]
```

This command prints the prime numbers between the start and stop values provided. Like the command factor, this probably isn't a command you'll use everyday. But the UNIX traditions do need to be maintained.

See also: factor

ps

```
ps [-edafl] [-t terminal] [-p proclist]
[-u uidlist] [-g grplist]
```

This command is used to display the status of processes. This is useful if you wish to find out if a process is still running or need to kill an out-of-control process.

```
$   ps

PID TTY TIME COMMAND

19550 ttyd00h 0:00 ps

2820 ttyd00h 0:02 ksh
```

Switches and Options:

-e	Prints information about all running processes.
-d	Prints information about all processes except group leaders.
-a	Prints information about all processes except group leaders and processes not running on a terminal.
-f	Prints a full listing.
-l	Prints more information about each process.
-t *terminal*	Lists only the processes associated with a *terminal*.
-p *proclist*	Lists information about processes whose PIDs are listed in the *proclist*.
-u *uidlist*	Lists processes owned by the UIDs specified in comma separated *uidlist*.
-g *grplist*	Lists processes specified by comma separated *grplist*.

pwd

```
pwd
```

This command displays the name of the current working directory.

```
$   pwd
    /users/jrice
```

rcp

```
rcp [-p] file1 file2

rcp [-p] [-r] file1 [file2 ...] directory
```

This command allows you to copy files between workstations on a network. File and directory specifications take the form of either *hostname:pathname* or just *pathname* for the local system. For instance,

```
$   rcp /test home:/test
```

copies the file test to the root level of the workstation named home.

Switches and Options:

-p   Gives each copy the same attributes (modification time, access time, mode) as the original, if possible.

-r   Copies all subdirectories.

Remarks and Cautions:

You must be listed as a valid remote user on the target host machine in order to make copies onto it.

See also: cp

reboot

```
reboot [-h | -r] [-n | -s] [-q]
[-t time] [-m message] [-d device]
[-f lif_filename]
[[-l serve_linkaddress] | [-b
boot_server]]
```

This command forces your workstation to start over from scratch. For instance,

$ reboot

forces a "quick" reboot of your computer. Current processes are not terminated first.

Switches and Options:

-h   Shuts the system down to a halt state.

-r   Causes the system to reboot automatically.

-n   Does not sync the filesystems before the shutdown is performed (bad).

-s   Syncs the filesystems before the shutdown is performed (good).

-q   Quick reboot. System does not attempt to kill current processes. It does not send any broadcast messages.

-t time   Specifies the time that the system will go down. This is time relative to the present time (+number of minutes) or an absolute time (hour:minute) based on a 24-hour clock or the word now.

-m message Broadcasts the message to all users on the system about the computer going down.

-d device   Reboots from the specified device.

-f *lif_filename* Specifies the *lif_filename* that the system will reboot from. (Supported on the series 300 and 400 systems only.)

-l *server_linkaddress*

Specifies the ethernet address that the computer will reboot from. This is the ethernet link address of a remote computer's ethernet interface.

-b *boot_server* Specifies the name of an active HP cluster server that can host the computer you are rebooting.

See also: shutdown

rlogin

```
rlogin hostname [-e c] [-7] [-8]
[-1 username]
```

Use this command to log onto another machine on your network. For instance,

```
$   rlogin server -1 jrice ↵
```

attempts to log user "jrice" onto the host machine named "server."

Switches and Options:

-e	Sets the escape character to c.
-8	Uses eight-bit data over the network, rather than seven-bit.
-7	Uses seven-bit data over the network, rather than eight-bit.
-1 *username*	Specifies alternative username. If this option is omitted, you are logged on under your current name.

Remarks and Cautions:

You must be running under a network to use this command.

See also: rcp

---

rm

rm [-f | -i] [-Rr] *filename* [...]

This command can be used to remove links, files, or directories. Files that are removed are not archived, so once they are removed, you'll need to retrieve them from a backup tape if you make an error.

$ rm trash

Switches and Options:

-r   Recursively removes all the directories and subdirectories. All files contained in the specified directory tree are also removed.

-R   Same as -r.

-f   Ignores the file modes, removes as much as possible without complaining.

-i   Interactive mode. Prompts the user before removing each file or directory.

Remarks and Cautions:

Use extreme caution when removing things. Since there are no methods short of restoring from backup tapes, rm can ruin your day very quickly. Check to make sure that you are in the directory that you think you are in. Check your command line before you hit <Enter>; rm -rf * .pay is not the same as *.pay.

rmdir

```
rmdir [-f|-i] [-p] dir...
```

This command removes a directory.

```
$   rmdir olddir
```

Switches and Options:

- f   Forces the removal of the directory without prompting or reporting of any errors.

- i   Writes a confirmation prompt out to standard error before actually removing the directory specified.

- p   Removes the directory dirname and any of its parent directories that are empty. rmdir stops removing parent directories when it encounters one that is not empty. When the rmdir command is finished it will print a message telling you that the directory was removed. If it is unable to remove a directory, it will print an error message explaining why.

rusers

rusers [-a] [-h] [-i] [l] [-u] *host...*

This command displays a list of all the users currently logged onto the specified hosts. If no host is specified, the entire network is canvassed.

Switches and Options:

-a   Reports for host even if no users are currently logged onto it.

-h   Sorts list alphabetically by host machine name.

-i   Sorts list by idle time.

-l   Outputs long format listing, such as that given by who command.

-u   Sorts list by number of users on each host.

Remarks and Cautions:

You must be running under a network to use this command. Also, remote hosts must be running the rusersd daemon, normally started from inetd.

See also: rlogin, rcp

shutdown

```
shutdown [-h | -r] [-d device]
[-f lif_file] [-y] [grace]
```

Shutdown is an administrative process used to halt, bring the system into single user mode for backups or kernal rebuilds, or reboot the computer.

Switches and Options:

-h	Shuts the system down to a halt state.
-r	Shuts down the system and reboots it automatically.
-d device	Reboots the computer from a specific device.
-f lif_file	Reboots the computer from a specific lif_ format file. (Supported on the series 300 and 400 systems only.)
-y	Does not require any user interaction in the reboot process.
grace	Specifies the grace period (in seconds) that users will have to logout before the system shuts down. The keyword now can be used in place of a 0 (zero).

⮞ **NOTE:** *If neither the -r or the -h switch is used, the system will be shut down to the single user mode.*

⮞ **NOTE:** *You must be the superuser or be given permission through the /etc/shutdown.allow file to use this command.*

See also: reboot

sort

```
sort [-cmu] [-o output] [-y kmem]
[-z recsz] [Tdir] [-tx] [-bdfilnrM]
[-k keydef] file ...

sort [-cmu] [-o output] [-y kmem]
[-z recsz] [Tdir] [-tx] [-bdfilnrM]
[+pos1 [-pos2]] file ...
```

This command sorts the given files' contents, sending the results to standard output (usually the screen).

Switches and Options:

-c	Checks first to see if the file has been sorted to specification; if so, sort will do nothing.
-m	Merges the files only. It assumes the input files are already sorted.
-u	Suppresses all but one of each line that has a unique sort key.
-o output	Uses output as the destination for the sorted file rather than the default standard out.
-y kmem	Defines the amount of memory for the sort to use. Systems limits are observed (-y 0 will use the smallest memory chunk, while -y uses the maximum allowed).
-z recsz	The largest record size in the files must be supplied if two files are to be merged and the largest record in the files to be merged is larger than the default system record size.
-Tdir	Uses the directory (dir) provided for temporary scratch space rather than the default /usr/tmp directory.
-d	Sorts using quasi-dictionary order.
-f	Folds letters prior to comparing them.

-i   Ignores nonprinting characters in the sort
            process.

-M   Compares the sort keys with month names
            and then sorts them in chronological order.
            Sort keys that can't be matched with month
            names are sorted before valid month names.
            (Invalid months are considered smallest.)

-n   Sorts based on initial numeric strings. The
            sort command will assume that the initial
            value in each line is a number. Values that
            can't be interpreted as numbers will be
            treated as zero.

-r   Reverses the sense of the comparisons.

-tx   Uses x as the field separator.

-b   Ignores leading blanks.

spell

```
spell [-v] [-b] [-x] [-l] [-i]
[+local_file] files
```

This command performs a spelling check on the indicated files. The system maintains an internal dictionary for this purpose. Misspelled words are echoed to the screen. For instance,

```
$ spell test.text
```

```
chpter
```

Switches and Options:

-b	Uses British spelling rules.
-i	Ignores certain formatting files.
-l	Follows chains of included files.
-v	Prints derived entries (those not literally on the list).
-x	Prints all plausible word stems for erroneous entries.
+local_file	Uses the named file as the appropriate spelling list.

split

```
split [-l line_count] [-a suffix_length]
filename

split [-b n[k|m]] [-a suffix_length]
filename
```

This command divides a given file into small files. The number of lines in each output file is specified by the value of `line_count`. If the `-l` option isn't provided, the default value of 1000 is used for the `line_count`.

The output filenames all begin with "name" and end with lexicographically increasing suffixes starting with "aa" and ending with "zz." For instance,

```
$   split myfile smaller
```

splits the input file `myfile` into a number of 1000-line-long files, each of whose names begins with "smaller." The first such file is `smalleraa`, the second `smallerab`, and so on.

Switches and Options:

`-l line_count` Splits file into segments that are all `line_count` lines in length.

`-a suffix_length` The `suffix_length` is used to determine the size of the suffix formed on the output filenames. This switch allows `split` to exceed the 676 output file limit that exists if only aa through zz could be used.

`-b n` Splits file into pieces that are _n_ bytes in size.

`-b nk` The file will be split into _n_ * 1 Kb in size.

`-b nm` The file will be split into _n_ * 1 Mb in size.

`-n` The input file is split into chunks _n_ lines in size. This option is obsolete and is replaced by the `-l` option.

SU

```
su [-] [username] [args ...]
```

This command re-logs you into the current shell as the desired user. If no user is specified, the desired user is assumed to be the superuser. For instance,

```
$   su root
Password:
```

After supplying the correct password, the user is logged in as the superuser.

Switches and Options:

- Using this switch causes the path to be reset and the /etc/profile and .profile to be executed.

args Additional *args* placed on the command line are passed directly to the shell process that's invoked.

Remarks and Cautions:

Superuser status is extremely powerful. You can do all kinds of damage. Knowledge of the superuser password should be restricted to those responsible for system maintenance.

See also: login, passwd

tail

```
tail [-b | -c | -1] [-f] [-n number] file
```

This command echoes the last part of the given file to the screen. If no filename is given, then the standard input is used.

Switches and Options:

-b
The quantity of output to be measured in 512-byte blocks.

-c
The quantity of output to be measured in characters.

-1
The quantity of output to be measured in lines. (This is the default.)

-f
The "follow" option. This option causes the tail command to enter an endless loop, watching for more information on the end of the file to be copied to the display.

-n number
The value of number indicates the quantity of specified units (blocks, bytes, or lines) to index into the file before beginning the output.

Positive numbers indicate an index relative to the beginning of the file. Negative numbers indicate a number relative to the end of the file.

tar

tar *key [arguments...]*
[file | -C directory]

This command creates and reads archive files that are
collections of directories and data files. These archives are
typically stored on magnetic media, such as tapes, but can
also be built as single data files. Archive files are in binary
(nonreadable) form. For example,

$ tar -cvf /dev/rmt/0m /users ⏎

creates an archive of the /users directory, storing it on a
tape attached to the system and referenced through the
device file /dev/rmt/0m.

Switches and Options:

-c	Creates new archive.
-r	Appends files to an existing archive.
-t	Prints the names of objects stored in the archive file.
-u	Adds files to archive only if not present, or if modified.
-x	Extracts files from named archive. **NOTE:** *Only one of the preceding options may be used.*
-N	Writes a new (POSIX) format archive.
-0	Writes an old (pre-POSIX) format archive.
-A	Suppresses a warning message that tar didn't store a files access control list. tar normally writes a warning message out about every file it archives with an acl , indicating that the acl couldn't be archived.
-b *number*	Uses block size of specified size.

-f *archivename* Stores or extracts files using given archive name. For storage, archive name is usually a device, such as /dev/rmt/0m for tape.

-h Follows symbolic links.

-H Causes all elements of a context-dependent file to be written to the archive.

-l Causes tar to complain if it can't resolve a symbolic link.

-m Tells tar not to restore the modification date written on the tape.

-o Asks tar not to write directory information that older versions of tar can't handle as input.

-p Causes file to be restored to its original mode and ownerships as written on the archive.

-#d Specifies a particular tape drive number (#) and the drive density (d).

-v Operates in verbose mode.

-V Similar to -v except that when -t is used, more information about the type of the archive is written to the display.

-w Causes tar to prompt the user for confirmation before taking an action on a file.

-C *directory* Causes tar to perform a chdir to the directory before writing the specified files. This allows multiple, seemingly unrelated directories to be collected into a single archive.

See also: cpio

telnet

`telnet` *hostname* `[`*port*`]`

This command establishes a remote connection to the specified host using the TELNET protocol. If no host is specified, system enters TELNET command mode. TELNET commands may be entered at this point; type ? for a list of these commands.

time

```
time [command arguments]
```

This command executes the given process and times it. Results returned include the total elapsed real time, the system time, and the process time.

umount

```
umount [-v] [-s] fsname

umount [-v] [-s] directory

umount -a [-v] [-s] [-h host] [-t type]
```

This command releases the indicated filesystem, so that it is no longer available. For instance,

```
$   umount /dev/dsk/c201d3s0 unmounts a disk
    available through the device file
    /dev/dsk/c201d3s0, regardless of what
    name the filesystem is mounted under.
```

Switches and Options:

-v	Verbose mode.
-t type	Unmounts only filesystems mounted as a given type.
-h host	Unmounts only those filesystems that have been NFS mounted from the remote system named host.
-s	Doesn't update the /etc/mnttab file. (Please don't use this option.)
-a	Unmounts all locally mounted filesystems that aren't busy and are described in the /etc/mnttab file.

Remarks and Cautions:

You must enter this command before you can eject a mounted floppy, magneto-optical disk, or CD-ROM.

See also: mount

uncompress

```
uncompress [-f] [-v] [-c] [-V]
filename ...
```

This command restores a file previously reduced in size by the compress command.

Switches and Options:

- f   Causes uncompress to complete without complaining about possible errors, even if the input file specified doesn't exist.

- v   Prints a message describing the compression ratio that was attained by the compressed file.

- c   Writes results to standard output without changing the source file.

- V   Writes the version and the compile options used by the uncompress program.

See also: compress, zcat

unexpand

unexpand [-a] *filename*

This command removes multiple spaces from a specified file and replaces them with tab characters. Results are copied to standard output.

Switches and Options:

-a   Replaces spaces with tabs only when this produces a smaller output file.

See also: expand

ux2dos

```
ux2dos file ...
```

This command converts files from UNIX to MS-DOS format. It is particularly useful for preparing text files for use on a DOS format machine. ux2dos reads the filenames provided on the command line and converts them to DOS format as it writes them to the display. If no filenames are given, ux2dos reads information from the standard input stream and converts it as it writes it back out to standard out. For instance,

```
$   ux2dos HOME/test.TXT $HOME/test.txt
```

converts the file test.TXT to a DOS format file named test.txt, storing it in my home directory.

See also: dos2ux

w

w [-hls] *username*

This command prints system usage summaries for the specified user or users. If no username is given, all users logged onto the local host are listed.

Switches and Options:

-h	Suppresses headers.
-l	Uses long format display.
-s	Uses short format display (default is long).

See also: who

who

```
who [-muTlHqpdbrtasAcR] file

who am i

who am I
```

This command displays a list of the current system users, finding out who is currently using the system, their terminal line, and the time that they logged into the system.

```
$  who
   jrice ttyp0 Jun 24 10:15 ()
   billb console Jun 23 09:31
```

Asking the system, "who am i" or "who am I," prints only your information,

```
$  who am i
   jrice ttyp0 Jun 24 10:15 ()
```

Switches and Options:

-m	Outputs information about users on the current terminal.
-u	Lists only those users who are currently logged on.
-T	Same as -u except that the state of the terminal is printed.
-l	Lists only those lines that are waiting for someone to login.
-H	Prints headings above each of the columns.
-q	A quick list of the users' names and the number of users who are logged in.
-p	Lists any other active processes that have been spawned by a system process called "init."

-d	Lists all expired processes that haven't been respawned by the system process called "init."
-b	Indicates the time and date of the last reboot.
-r	Indicates the current run level of the system.
-t	Indicates the last change of the system clock by root using the `date` command.
-a	Executes with all options turned on.
-s	The default listing of all current username, line, and time fields.
-A	When using `/etc/wtmp`, this indicates when the accounting system was turned on or off.
-c	Displays information about the entire HP cluster.
-R	Displays the user's hostname.

whoami

```
whoami
```

This command displays who is logged in to this terminal. For instance,

```
$    whoami
     root
```

yppasswd

yppasswd *name*

This command is used to change a user's password on the system using the Network Information Services (formerly called Yellow Pages). Users are only allowed to change their own passwords. A superuser is allowed to change the password of another user on the network.

Switches and Options:

name   This option can be used by the superuser to change the password of a user.

See also: passwd

zcat

zcat *file* ...

This command uncompresses given files, sending results to standard output without modifying the original file. This command is functionally equivalent to uncompress -c.

See also: compress, uncompress

Index

More
OnWord Press Titles

Pro/ENGINEER Books

INSIDE Pro/ENGINEER
Book $49.95 Includes Disk

**The Pro/ENGINEER Quick
Reference**
Book $24.95

**The Pro/ENGINEER Exercise
Book**
Book $39.95 Includes Disk

Interleaf Books

INSIDE Interleaf
Book $49.95 Includes Disk

**Adventurer's Guide to
Interleaf Lisp**
Book $49.95 Includes Disk

The Interleaf Exercise Book
Book $39.95 Includes Disk

The Interleaf Quick Reference
Book $24.95

Interleaf Tips and Tricks
Book $49.95 Includes Disk

MicroStation Books

**INSIDE MicroStation 5X
3d edition**
Book $34.95 Includes Disk

**MicroStation Reference
Guide 5.X**
Book $18.95

MicroStation Exercise Book
Book $34.95
Optional Instructor's Guide $14.95

**The MicroStation
Productivity Book**
Book $39.95
Optional Disk $49.95

MicroStation Bible
Book $49.95
Optional Disk $49.95

Programming With MDL
Book $49.95
Optional Disk $49.95

Programming With User Commands
Book $65.00
Optional Disk $40.00

101 MDL Commands
Book $49.95
Optional Executable Disk $101.00
Optional Source Disks (6)
$259.95

101 User Commands
Book $49.95
Optional Disk $101.00

Bill Steinbock's Pocket MDL Programmer's Guide
Book $24.95

MicroStation for AutoCAD Users
Book $29.95 Optional Disk $14.95

MicroStation for AutoCAD Users Tablet Menu
Tablet Menu $99.95

MicroStation 5.X Delta Book
Book $19.95

Managing and Networking MicroStation
Book $29.95
Optional Disk $29.95

The MicroStation Database Book
Book $29.95
Optional Disk $29.95

The MicroStation Rendering Book
Book $34.95 Includes Disk

INSIDE I/RAS B
Book $24.95 Includes Disk

The CLIX Workstation User's Guide
Book $34.95 Includes Disk

Build Cell
Software $69.95

SunSoft Solaris Series

The SunSoft Solaris 2.* User's Guide
Book $29.95 Includes Disk

SunSoft Solaris 2.* for Managers and Administrators
Book $34.95
Optional Disk $29.95

The SunSoft Solaris 2.* Quick Reference
Book $18.95

Five Steps to SunSoft Solaris 2.*
Book $24.95 Includes Disk

One Minute SunSoft Solaris
Manager
Book $14.95

SunSoft Solaris 2.* for
Windows Users
Book $24.95

Windows NT

Windows NT for the Technical Professional
Book $29.95

The Hewlett Packard HP-UX Series

The HP-UX User's Guide
Book $29.95 Includes Disk

Five Steps to HP-UX
Book $24.95 Includes Disk

HP-UX For Managers and
Administrators
Book $34.95
Optional Disk $29.95

One Minute HP-UX Manager
Book $14.95

HP-UX for Windows Users
Book $24.95

The HP-UX Quick Reference
Book $18.95

CAD Management

One Minute CAD Manager
Book $14.95

Manager's Guide to
Computer-Aided Engineering
Book $49.95

Other CAD

CAD and the Practice of
Architecture: ASG Solutions
Book $39.95 Includes Disk

Using Drafix Windows CAD
Book $34.95 Includes Disk

INSIDE CADVANCE
Book $34.95 Includes Disk

Fallingwater in 3D Studio: A
Case Study and Tutorial
Book $39.95 Includes Disk

Geographic Information Systems

The GIS Book. 3d edition
Book $34.95

DTP/CAD Clip Art

1001 DTP/CAD Symbols Clip
Art Library: Architectural
Book $29.95

DISK FORMATS:
MicroStation
DGN Disk $175.00
Book/Disk $195.00

AutoCAD
DWG Disk $175.00
Book/Disk $195.00

CAD/DTP
DXF Disk $195.00
Book/Disk $225.00

Networking/LANtastic

Fantastic LANtastic
Book $29.95 Includes Disk

The LANtastic Quick
Reference
Book $14.95

One Minute Network Manager
Book $14.95

OnWord Press Distribution

End Users/User Groups/Corporate Sales

OnWord Press books are available worldwide to end users, user groups, and corporate accounts from your local bookseller or computer/software dealer, or from HMP Direct: call 1-800-526-BOOK or 505-473-5454; fax 505-471-4424; write to High Mountain Press Direct, 2530 Camino Entrada, Santa Fe, NM 87505-8435, or e-mail to ORDERS@BOOKSTORE.HMP.COM.

Wholesale, Including Overseas Distribution

We have international distributors. Contact us for your local source by calling 1-800-4-ONWORD or 505-473-5454; fax to 505-471-4424; e-mail to ORDERS@BOOKSTORE.HMP.COM; or write to High Mountain Press/IPG, 2530 Camino Entrada, Santa Fe, NM 87505-8435, USA.

Comments and Corrections

Your comments can help us make better products. If you find an error in our products, or have any other comments, positive or negative, we'd like to know! Please write to us at the address below or contact our e-mail address: READERS@ HMP.COM.

OnWord Press
2530 Camino Entrada, Santa Fe, NM 87505-8435 USA